Praise for Drs. John and Julie Gottman
and *The Love Prescription*

"The Gottmans are the nation's leading marriage researchers and educators."
—Time

"John and Julie Gottman are the renowned experts on marital stability."
—The Atlantic

"The Einstein of Love."
—Psychology Today

"The dean of marriage experts."
—The New York Times

PENGUIN LIFE

THE LOVE PRESCRIPTION

John Gottman, PhD, was voted one of the Top 10 Most Influential Therapists of the past quarter century and was recently honored with the 2021 Lifetime Achievement Award by *Psychotherapy Networker*. Professor emeritus in psychology at the University of Washington, Dr. Gottman is known for his work on marital stability and relationship analysis through scientific direct observations, self-report, and physiology. He is the author or coauthor of more than two hundred published academic articles and more than forty-five books, including the bestselling *The Seven Principles for Making Marriage Work*, *What Makes Love Last?*, *The Relationship Cure*, and *Why Marriages Succeed or Fail*. He is a cofounder of The Gottman Institute and of Affective Software, Inc., which has created a teletherapy technology that will live on cell phones, computers, and tablets to assist therapists in couples therapy and offer relationship-building services directly to couples.

Julie Schwartz Gottman, PhD, cofounder and president of The Gottman Institute and cofounder of Affective Software, Inc., was recently honored with the 2021 Lifetime Achievement Award by *Psychotherapy Networker* for decades of work revolutionizing couples therapy. Winner of the Washington State Distinguished Psychologist of the Year, she has coauthored seven books, including the popular *10 Principles for Doing Effective Couples Therapy*, *And Baby Makes Three*, and *Eight Dates*. She is also the cocreator of the immensely popular The Art and Science of Love weekend workshop for couples and codesigner of the Gottman Method Couples Therapy clinical training program, which she has taught nationally and in more than fifteen countries.

THE LOVE PRESCRIPTION

Seven Days to More Intimacy, Connection, and Joy

JOHN GOTTMAN, PhD, AND
JULIE SCHWARTZ GOTTMAN, PhD

life

Rx

PENGUIN BOOKS
An imprint of Penguin Random House LLC
penguinrandomhouse.com

A Penguin Life Book

LIBRARY OF CONGRESS CATALOGING-IN-PUBLICATION DATA
Names: Gottman, John Mordechai, author. | Gottman, Julie Schwartz, author.
Title: The love prescription : seven days to more intimacy, connection, and joy /
    John Gottman, PhD, and Julie Schwartz Gottman, PhD.
Description: First edition. | New York : Penguin Books, 2022. |
    Includes bibliographical references.
Identifiers: LCCN 2022006721 (print) | LCCN 2022006722 (ebook) |
    ISBN 9780143136637 (paperback) | ISBN 9780525508137 (ebook)
Subjects: LCSH: Love. | Interpersonal attraction.
Classification: LCC BF575.L8 .G664 2022 (print) | LCC BF575.L8 (ebook) |
    DDC 152.4/1—dc23/eng/20220701
LC record available at https://lccn.loc.gov/2022006721
LC ebook record available at https://lccn.loc.gov/2022006722

Printed in the United States of America
5th Printing

Book design by Daniel Lagin

Some names and identifying characteristics have been changed to protect the
privacy of the individuals involved.

We dedicate this book to our dear friends and colleagues Alan and Etana Kunovsky, who cofounded and built the Gottman Institute with us. It has been a wonderful journey.

CONTENTS

INTRODUCTION

SMALL THINGS OFTEN

LOVE. IT'S A BIG WORD—HARD TO DEFINE AND PIN DOWN. FOR CENTU-
ries, the poets have been trying. It's like a red, red rose (Burns).
Or it is an ever-fixed mark, that looks on tempests and is never
shaken (Shakespeare). It's a many-splendored thing (says one
classic romantic movie); it's never having to say you're sorry
(according to another). Can something so huge, so essential, so
mysterious, so individual—have a formula? Is there a "prescription" for love?

In a word: Yes.

And the most important thing to know about "the love prescription" is that it's a small one. Tiny little doses, every day, is
what it takes to make a healthy relationship. Why? Because that's
exactly what a relationship is—not one big thing, but a million
tiny things, every day, for a lifetime.

We should know: For the past fifty years, we've been putting
love under the microscope, starting with John's earliest research
on marital interactions at Indiana University and spanning to

today, as we still work closely with couples through the Gottman Institute. When we founded the Love Lab in Seattle in 1990, we wanted to know: What makes love last? Why does one couple stay together forever, while another falls apart? And was it even possible to quantify any of this with data—to use the tools of science and mathematical modeling to predict whether a couple would live happily ever after?

Since then, we've brought all kinds of couples—married and unmarried, gay and straight, couples with kids and those without, newlyweds and married-for-decades seasoned pros—into the lab to drill down to the key factors that make a good relationship good. We've looked at every facet of their relationships—their body language, the way they converse, the way they fight, their personal histories and their love stories; we've watched their heart rates rise and fall and measured the flood of stress hormones in their bodies. We've filmed their every movement and reviewed the footage down to the hundredth of a second. Every scrap of data that could be gathered, we collected. We lifted the lid on love and took out all the little parts to determine what, precisely, made it tick. Like the Hadron Collider smashing apart an atom, we wanted to see if we could isolate the building blocks of love.

And what did we learn, when we brought love into the lab?

Well, a lot. This has been our life's work. And this little book will offer you just a slice of it. But we think that in many ways, it's the most important slice. In this bite-sized, seven-day action plan, we'll be taking you through our most foundational findings—the first steps toward building a love that lasts. And here's the preview: love is a practice. More than a feeling, it's an action. It's something you do, not something that just happens to you. And you need to give—and get—a daily dose to maintain a healthy, thriving relationship.

The surprising thing is, it's not about grand gestures. It's not a Valentine's Day bouquet or a last-minute trip to Paris. It's not John Cusack standing outside your bedroom window with a boom box. Instead, it's all about little things done often. You've heard the expression "The devil is in the details"? Well, in relationships, the love is in the details. They're easy to do, but too often forgotten. We've all heard the phrase "Don't sweat the small stuff." It might be good life advice, but when it comes to love, it's 100 percent wrong. Love is all about the small stuff. And it's time to sweat.

The Rock That Changed the Course of a River

Mark and Annette had decided to separate. It wasn't an easy decision—they'd been married for more than a decade and had an eight-year-old daughter. But something was definitely off, and it had been for a long time. There had been a slow waning of attraction, interest, companionship. Their marriage had become dull and stale. They didn't look forward to seeing each other at the end of the day as they once had; somehow, most of their interactions now ended with tension or sniping, not sweetness. At best, they felt like business partners or roommates, not lovers or friends.

As a last-ditch effort, Mark suggested going to a therapist.

They hadn't tried this before. But Annette figured, why not? They didn't have anything to lose.

The therapist listened to their story. He asked them what they thought was wrong, and why they wanted to separate. Over a series of weekly sessions, the reasons came out: *Not getting along. No sex. Seems like all we do is fight.*

And then one week he said, "I have a weekend assignment for you."

He told them that he wanted them to do something outside their comfort zone. By their own description, Mark and Annette were fairly fastidious people—they liked keeping their home spotless and highly organized. Cleanliness was a top priority for them. Their daughter kept her toys neatly put away at all times; in their home, there wasn't a thing out of place. So the assignment the therapist gave them was this: Go out into your backyard and have a mud fight.

The couple was baffled. *A what?*

"A mud fight," the therapist insisted. "Get the hose out, make a mud pit, put on some old clothes, and get right in there. Throw mud at each other, just go for it!"

At home, the couple shook their heads and sighed. It was too bad that this therapist had turned out to be an idiot. They would have to find a new one.

Their daughter, who'd been listening in, had a different opinion.

"I think it's a great idea!" she chimed in.

They just shook their heads. Kids! The weekend rolled around, and they were feeling—as usual—disconnected and tense. In their shining, clean kitchen, drinking coffee, they talked it over: Give up on therapy? Start the search over and find a new therapist? Again, their daughter jumped in. "Let's have that mud fight!" she cried. "C'mon, do it! Just try it!"

She wouldn't let up. If you have kids, or know any, you understand how persistent they can be—and *loud*. Mark and Annette threw their hands up. "Fine, fine," they said. "You win." They got on some old clothes. Mark dug up a T-shirt he'd gotten at a concert years ago when they were still dating, except now his hair was graying and the shirt was a little snug around the middle; Annette ended up in an old, stained blouse, long out of style. They both felt ridiculous, hovering there in the backyard while the hose ran cold water into a pile of garden muck. But their daughter was looking at them expectantly, excitedly, and what else were they supposed to do? Mark bent down, grabbed a handful of cold gunk, but then hesitated. Annette took that moment to flick mud his way. It freckled his cheek. Now provoked, he threw his handful at her; she shrieked and scooped up some more; their daughter scooped up huge handfuls, and before long, it was a full-on mud war. Soon, they were howling with laughter, flinging mud everywhere, slipping, sliding, and rolling in it. They ended up with their arms around each other, laughing and kissing. They'd never felt closer. Or . . . grosser.

That mud fight completely turned around their relationship. Just a few moments in time—yet it had an enormous impact. From that moment on, Mark and Annette decided to make more time for fun and adventure in their family. Their experience reminded us of how a river can change its entire course from a single rock falling into it midstream. In circling around the rock, the river courses higher up its bank, carving out a new path for itself through sand, clay, and rock. Geologists have found that over time, rivers can even sculpt out new valleys in this way—all because of one tiny change.

Into the Love Lab

Mark and Annette shared this story and more when they came into the Love Lab to participate in one of our studies. When we observed them, it was clear that they had managed to re-create a strong and loving marriage. After so many years of in-tensive research, we can observe a couple for fifteen minutes and predict, with 90 percent accuracy, whether they'll stay together or not . . . *and* if that union will be a happy one.[1] And we could see, Mark and Annette were now in it for the long haul.

Long before we founded the Gottman Institute, John started out as a mathematician, fascinated by the ways that numbers could predict important truths about the world. But while do-ing graduate work at MIT, he found himself more interested in his roommate's psychology books than his own. He switched paths. And then, after spending a couple of decades researching relationships, that old love of math resurfaced. He started to wonder about the mathematics of love. After all, mathematical biologists had been able to model all sorts of things, from pan-demics to tumor formation to why tigers have stripes and leop-ards have spots. Why not love?

One of the first things that John discovered in the Love Lab was that we're often wrong about what makes love last. By tracking his theories and results over time, he found that 60 percent of his earliest ideas about what makes marriages succeed or fail were off base. Like the rest of us, he'd spawned those ideas from cultural stereotypes—our favorite novels, TV shows and movies, our own families and experiences. These all have the capacity to lead us astray, and often do. That's why we really need *data*. Analyzing data can accurately reveal what's true and not true about what helps relationships succeed. Fortunately, even with that dismal early record of poor predictions, John didn't quit. With his best friend, Dr. Robert Levenson, and his wife, Dr. Julie Schwartz Gottman, he dedicated his career to collecting and analyzing data to discover truths. The results? There *is* a science of love. And best of all, we now know clear ways to help a relationship. Love is—after all this time—no longer such a mystery.

We've studied more than three thousand couples in the Love Lab, following some for as long as twenty years, and we've studied more than forty thousand couples about to begin couples therapy. We've watched countless hours of tape. Aggregated millions of data points. And what we've discovered is that there are universal factors that make or break a relationship, that predict whether a couple will stay together happily, or not.

First, a couple needs to stay curious about each other. We all grow and change over time. Successful couples know this and take the time to make and expand their "love maps"—their knowledge of each other's inner worlds. That means not only asking questions, but also asking the right kind of questions.

Second, the couple needs to share fondness and admiration.

That means, among other things, seeing and appreciating the good things your partner does, finding and focusing on the things you admire about them, and expressing these things out loud or with touch. A lot of people think their partner already knows they're loved and admired—but what we've observed is that they don't. Loving words need to be said aloud much more often than we realize. This isn't the single drink of water you give your potted plant every few days, but the continuous oxygen you breathe.

And third, the couple turns toward each other instead of turning away. That means they make and respond to what we call "bids for connection." Bids can range from little things, like calling each other's names, to big things, like asking for deeper needs to be met. Successful couples are savvy enough to notice when their partner is making a bid, and they drop what they're doing, if necessary, to engage.

These are the factors that separate the "masters" of love from the disasters. And further, the masters understand that it's the small things you do (or don't do) on a daily basis that can make or break a relationship—because these are what create intimacy. It doesn't take much to turn a relationship around. It takes a question or two—the right kind. It takes a thank-you, or a real, genuine compliment. It takes giving your partner a chance to do something for you. It takes a six-second kiss. It takes . . . a handful of mud.

You might notice a few things conspicuously absent from the above list. Most notably, *conflict*.

Of course, conflict is a part of any close relationship. But when a relationship is on the rocks, or even just cooling off a bit, a major conflict is the last place you want to start. We're not saying you should ignore your problems. We're just saying it's not the place to begin. We know from the lab that the best relationships aren't built on partners mostly telling each other what's wrong. They're built on partners mostly telling each other what's *right*. So whether you're going through a rough patch, or just starting out and wondering what points of friction lie ahead, one thing we're not going to do here is have you sit down at the table, work on your conflict management skills, or workshop your Big Issues. We're going to tell you to first go out in the backyard, make a mud pit, and have a little fun.

We promise we'll make this easy for you. In the course of the next week, you can shift the culture of your relationship for the better—and you can do it in small, immediately actionable steps. For the next seven days, this will be your motto: *Small things often.*

This is Relationships 101. Nobody takes this class in high school or college (though we should!). We're left to learn how to have relationships from watching our parents, or TV and movies. And that's not always a good curriculum. It took us all these years to figure out the formula for a good relationship, and in the seven days that follow, we're going to dispense our best, most distilled and potent advice.

Anyone can do this, from any starting point. Julie, in her practice, has worked one-on-one with those in the most challenging circumstances that you can imagine: war vets with PTSD, heroin addicts, cancer survivors, and communities in deep poverty.

It's hard, and heartbreaking. And she loves it. It's work that portrays the incredible resilience of the human soul—people emerging from darkness into places of light. In the Love Lab, she's seen the same thing in relationships. There may be no embers left—just ash. And yet, you blow a little bit and *whoosh*! Up springs a fire.

HOW TO USE THIS BOOK

EACH OF THE CHAPTERS THAT FOLLOW IS GOING TO ASK YOU TO INTRO-
duce one new, relationship-building habit into your day, every day
for one week. Seven days, seven new habits. They'll be easy. They'll
be quick. They'll be fun. There will be no grand gestures and no
big, hard conversations. There are no requirements for when and
where you do these exercises with your person. These can be done
at any time of day, on the busiest of days; they can be done while
you put away the dishes, while driving in the car. There's nothing
to buy, or do, or prepare. You can start immediately.

But before we start, we want to address a few questions you
may have about this book, how to use it, and what to expect.

Is It Too Soon?

If you've just met someone you're interested in, you might be
wondering if it's too early to bring in an "intervention." There
is no *too soon* to introduce these "best practices" for love. *The*

sooner the better. Most couples wait much too long to seek help—an average of four to six years. By the time they come to see us, they're so far down the wrong path that it takes quite a lot of effort for us to help them find their way back out of the woods. We often think: *If only we'd gotten to you earlier!*

There's a misconception out there that you only need help with your relationship if you're having problems. But that's not how most of us behave in the other arenas of our lives. With everything from our bodies to our careers to, well, our *cars*, we are proactive—we try to eat right and exercise; we take our cars in for tune-ups *before* they break down. Why don't we think about relationships the same way?

It's *smart* to start early—to keep any relationship as healthy and well oiled as possible. If this is a brand-new relationship, you might not even know yet if this is the person you want to spend the rest of your life with—and that's OK! You don't need to be 100 percent sure; you just need to know that you want to find out. The data in this book—culled from the most successful relationships we've studied—are going to help you get started on the right foot . . . and then keep going in the right direction.

Is It Too Late?

If you're coming to this book in a particularly rocky period for your marriage or partnership, you might be wondering if the window to turn things around has passed. Your problems may feel complicated and deeply entrenched. You might be finding it hard to see your way out.

We can tell you this: In all of our years of research and office practice, it has been very rare that we encounter couples for whom it is truly "too late." Most couples wait an average of *six years* of being unhappy before they seek help.[1] Whether you've been noticing problems for a week or a decade—we can help. The only thing that really spells the end of a relationship is if you've both already thrown in the towel. And if you're holding this book, we're willing to bet that isn't the case.

We said that we can predict with 90 percent accuracy whether a couple will stay together or not, and if it'll be a happy union—but that's not written in stone. We can't literally see the future. We simply make our best guess based on the *patterns* we observe. When people change those unhealthy patterns to healthy ones, they can change their future.

You might think that the couples who are most unhappy at the beginning of an intervention will benefit the least—that they won't be able to catch up. But it's just not true. Our research (and the research of others in the field) shows that couples who are struggling the most actually make the most gains. Everyone can benefit. And if you're in a rocky patch, you actually stand to change the most.

In short: *It's not too late to strengthen your relationship.*

What If My Partner Isn't Enthusiastic about Doing This with Me?

It would be great if you both read along together. But this is real life, and things don't always go according to the ideal! If you're the primary partner reading this book, share with your partner the most interesting tidbits from each chapter—something like, "Hey, did you know that couples who cuddle have the most sex?" is sure to get their attention.

Tell them this: The exercises are easy. Most can be done in just a few minutes. And they're *fun.* Tell your partner that these are all ways to increase passion, connection, and good sex—and to bring a little more lightness and love into the house. We could all use that, no matter how great our partnerships are already.

Can I Really Change My Relationship in Just One Week?

When we were running the Love Lab, we had plenty of success working with couples and tailoring a fleet of interventions for them to try. But we wondered: What if couples couldn't take off for a whole weekend of workshops? Could we still make a difference?

So we ran an experiment (with the help of *Reader's Digest* and the writer Joan DeClaire). We brought couples in. They did a full relationship assessment that all couples did who came into the office—exhaustive questionnaires that got into every nook and cranny of their relationship. Then, we sent them off to lunch.

While they went to get a sandwich, we met with our staff to pore over their answers, evaluate the data, and choose *one single* intervention that we could do with them in an hour. For instance, training them to positively express their needs without criticizing their partner. When they came back, we did the one intervention we'd chosen. Then, we waited . . . two years.

After those two years, Joan followed up with all the couples. What she found was a staggering success rate for that single intervention. By and large, these couples had changed their dynamic. And they stayed changed two years later.[2]

Yes, we pinpointed the intervention that we guessed would be most helpful. But it was striking that one single shift in the way a couple interacted could have this much of an impact on their relationship, and on their lives.

Can these small shifts in habits that we recommend here really change your relationship?

Yes.

We're in Love. Isn't That Enough?

That's easy. *No.*

Love is not enough. Because so often, as time goes on, we stop courting each other. We stop prioritizing romance, fun, adventure, and great sex. Life gets in the way. In a study of thirty dual-career couples, the Sloan Center for Working Families at UCLA discovered that relationships often become just endless to-do lists; conversation becomes constrained to errands and planning.[3] In other words, you need to intentionally *practice* these aspects of the relationship that we'll lay out for you.

These practices will help you if you're dating and wondering what's next, or if you've been married fifty years. This is for any age, any stage. This is our starter kit for a great start, a restart, or a course correction. And all you need in order to begin is a willingness to try.

DAY 1

MAKE CONTACT

ALISON AND JEREMY SHOWED UP FOR ONE OF OUR WEEKEND COUPLES retreats looking tired. It wasn't surprising: we already knew from their intake forms that they had young kids and had been working from home, while supervising remote learning, for months. Of course they looked exhausted.

It was nine months into the COVID-19 pandemic, and like everything, the retreat was on Zoom. Not being in the same physical space with our participants, we had to work especially hard to observe their emotional states and body language. But even through the slightly grainy, brightly pixelated Zoom window, we could see Alison and Jeremy's disconnect. They sat side by side so that we could see them both through our screen, but they could have been in their own separate Zoom squares, sitting in different rooms, miles apart.

Alison and Jeremy explained why they'd enrolled: They felt constantly at odds with each other. They always seemed to disagree on how to handle stuff—everything from how to deal with a kid not wanting to finish his vegetables to how much risk they were comfortable taking on during the pandemic. Should they see friends outside, or not gather at all? Should they require the kids to wear masks if they went for a bike ride in the neighborhood? Everything turned into a fight; then life intervened before they could resolve it—the kids burst in, or an urgent work issue came up (work had seemingly become a twenty-four-hour activity, now that everything was remote)—and they would end up ruminating on the fight and just getting more upset. They were having thoughts they never used to have about the other: *He never really considers my opinion; he just thinks of reasons why I'm wrong. She always pushes her agenda; she always has to win.*

"We used to be more in sync," Alison said. "I mean, with little kids, there's always been a lot of logistics and dropped balls. But now we're just never on the same page."

We asked them to describe a typical day. When did they have opportunities to connect? Not to problem solve or work through life logistics—but to talk and listen.

They blinked at us.

"We don't have any," Jeremy replied. They hit the ground running in the morning, one of them taking work calls in a bedroom while the other got the kids fed and ready for remote school; one or both of them usually ended up skipping lunch in lieu of squeezing in some work time. Dinner was chaos; then one of them was cleaning up while the other did bedtime. Jeremy said, "By the time I finish doing the dishes and come upstairs, she's already asleep."

We don't need to be mid-pandemic for this to sound familiar. And you don't need to have kids underfoot to feel like it's hard to make time to connect.

Here's a massive misconception that a lot of us have: For connection to be meaningful, you must give hours of time to it. Therefore, in a busy day, we just don't have time for it. True?

False.

We have opportunities for meaningful connection constantly—but we miss them. We don't know exactly what we're looking for, and we don't know how important these seemingly small, fleeting, insignificant moments can be. In the language of the science of love, what we are doing in these quick moments is making what we call "bids for connection."

What's a bid for connection? Well, it can look like a casual remark. It can be as simple as one person sitting down next to the other one. It can be as subtle as a sigh. It's an *invitation to connect.* And how we respond to these tiny bids for connection can actually make or break a relationship! This was one of our first and most foundational discoveries in the Love Lab.

Bids for Connection: The Biggest Predictor of Happiness

We built our first Love Lab in an apartment on the shores of Montlake, near the University of Washington's red brick, cherry tree–lined campus. For a lab, it was unusually comfortable. When people walked into it, we didn't want them to feel like they were in a science lab. We wanted them to feel at home.

Julie designed the lab with that in mind—there were paintings on the walls, comfy furniture and cozy throws, a fully stocked kitchen. There was music to listen to and television to watch. The large picture windows framed the lake, smooth and shimmering in the sun (it doesn't actually rain here as much as people think it does—don't tell anybody; it's Seattle's little secret!). At night, the skyline of Downtown glittered, punctuated by the Space Needle's famous silhouette. If you didn't know any better, you'd think you were walking into any thoughtfully appointed Airbnb. You'd drop your bags and head out for a night on the town. But if you were coming to the Love Lab, you weren't going out. You were there so we could watch you. You might have noticed three cameras mounted to the walls throughout the apartment—we'd figured out that was how many we needed in order to visually monitor the entire space with no blind spots.

Our first big study had 130 newlywed couples visit the Love Lab, one couple at a time. These were couples who were truly in the "honeymoon" period—the months immediately following their wedding. We gave them absolutely no instructions. We just settled them there for the weekend and let them do whatever they would normally do. People watched their favorite shows, they read newspapers, they cooked meals, they cleaned up, they talked, they fought. We watched and recorded *everything*. We tracked even the smallest behavioral patterns. Everything was coded.

We weren't sure exactly what we were looking for—at that point, we didn't know which specific behaviors might turn out to be significant or predictive of future happiness or distress.

We just knew that we had to watch closely and code it all so we could find out.

Pretty quickly, a pattern emerged surrounding what we started calling bids for connection. One person would make a bid, initiating a moment of connection—it could be physical or verbal, overt or subtle—and the researcher controlling the camera would zoom in close on their partner's faces. Partners responded to bids for connection in one of three ways:

1. By **turning toward**: They gave a positive or affirmative response, acknowledging the other person and engaging with their attempt to connect. (Even a "hmm?" can count as turning toward.)
2. By **turning away**: They gave no response, either actively ignoring or just not noticing their partner's attempt to connect.
3. By **turning against**: They responded irritably or angrily to actively shut down their partner's attempt to connect.

What do each of these look like in practice?

Let's use this example:

Your partner, scrolling on their phone, remarks, "Oh, this is an interesting article." ← *bid for connection*

Here are your possible responses:

a. You look up and say, "Oh yeah? What's it about?" ← *turning toward*
b. You keep typing the email you're working on while staring at your screen. ← *turning away*

   c. You say, "Be quiet! Can't you see I'm trying to work?!" ← *turning against*

Sometimes, our bids for connection can look negative or hard to read, and we fail to interpret them as an attempt to connect. Let's look at another, perhaps less obvious, example:

You're sitting quietly at dinner. You give a deep audible sigh. (That's the bid.) Here's how your partner might respond:

   a. Your partner says, "Hey, honey, is something the matter? You sound tired." ← *turning toward*

   b. Your partner is reading the paper; they turn the page and say nothing. ← *turning away*

   c. Your partner says, "What's the matter *now*?! ← *turning against*

In the lab (and in real life!), no couples "turn toward" 100 percent of the time. But whether you turn toward a lot or a little really matters . . . a *lot*. We followed our 130 newlyweds for years—through their honeymoon months, first pregnancies, births of their babies, and beyond. We saw happiness for some couples, unhappiness for others, and for still others, divorce. Six years later, when we looked back on the data to see what coded behavior had been significant, we found something huge. The couples who got divorced had only turned toward their partner's bids 33 percent of the time. The couples who stayed together had turned toward 86 percent of the time.[1] It was an enormous difference—a statistical gap you rarely see in scientific studies.

We'd found a major point of intervention. If we could help couples understand the importance of these little moments that might seem like nothing, just slipping by under the radar, we could really help people turn things around. How people reacted to their partner's bids for connection was in fact the biggest predictor of happiness and relationship stability. These fleeting little moments, it turned out, spelled the difference between happiness and unhappiness, between lasting love and divorce.

Turning Toward:
The Number One Relationship Hack

We run a two-day workshop for couples where Day 1 is focused on *friendship and intimacy*, and Day 2 is focused on *conflict*. Of course, the point of the workshop is that couples tackle *both* of these essential topics. But we wondered: Which was more urgent? If couples wanted to start with the most impactful interventions, what would help them the most?

So, we did an experimental study: One group of participants just did Day 1, another group only did Day 2, and the final group did both days. One year later, we recontacted the couples. How was everybody doing?

It's probably no big shocker that the group that did both days of the workshop had retained the most *lasting changes* after a year. But interestingly, the group that only did Day 1 was also doing pretty well! On the other hand, the group that only did

Day 2—*conflict only*—fared the worst.[2] The message was clear: Focusing only on conflict was the wrong way to go about things. **First, we have to work on friendship.**

That's hard to do, because if you *are* in conflict, you may have a strong desire to "fix" it. But when we gravitate back to our conflicts first, we can make things worse. Why? Because as tensions rise, our bodies can respond physiologically; we can get overwhelmed and default to our old habitual ways of coping. For example, even after all these years in a loving and rewarding marriage, John has to fight against being immediately defensive. And Julie's first instinct when things get heated is to run out the door and into the nearest forest.

It's extremely hard to change the way people act during conflict. But with turning toward, you're changing how people act in the little moments that happen every day. That's much easier to do. And it will eventually help with conflict. We discovered that the more turning toward there is in a relationship, the better couples are at managing their conflicts. Even when conflict goes south, a couple's capacity to course correct and repair their interaction is *based on* how much they've turned toward each other in the past. With more turning toward, there's more shared humor, even during conflict. More lightness. More capacity to pause in the middle of a fight and make a peace offering, and more likelihood that that repair attempt will be received and reciprocated. Successful couples don't fight *less* than other couples—they fight better. And turning toward is the single biggest predictor of this.

What turning toward really does is put money in a couple's

emotional bank account. Think of every act of turning toward your partner's bid for connection—even one as simple and fleeting as responding to a smile with a smile—as dropping a coin in your love piggy bank.

When we were first married—thirty-four years ago now!—there was something we were better at then than we are now: building a grudge.

Maybe you know what we mean. A conversation gets a bit heated, your partner hurts your feelings, and you withdraw and start building a grudge against them—a litany of all the other ways they have wronged you recently, or since the beginning of time. John thinks back to the early years of their marriage and recalls how *actively* he would build a grudge—like building a chair, you have to cut the rough materials of your life down to fit it, bang it together, shape it, and sit on it. He and Julie would have a fight or a tiff and, feeling wounded, he'd disappear to do his grudge building. But in a relationship with a lot of turning toward, you hit a point where you go off to build your grudge, but then, you just . . . *can't*. John would be sitting there, trying his darndest to put together a durable, sturdy grudge, and there would be this annoying voice in his head. *Remember last week when you were sick and she came up to check on you and brought you tea? Remember this morning when she laughed at your joke? Remember earlier today when she went to the trouble to make you lunch, even though she was so busy? When she asked you later how your day was going? Those moments were all pretty nice.* He just couldn't build that grudge anymore.

As you accumulate all these moments of positivity and

connection, they offset the negative ones. A grudge just can't grow. Every single moment is emotional money in the bank. So when you hit a moment of conflict or tension, you have a *lot* in your "emotional bank account" to draw on. Even in a thorny moment that could be fertile ground for miscommunication and hurt feelings, you have all this positivity and connection banked, so you're more able to meet your partner with empathy and even humor. And the way you make positive deposits into your bank account is through turning toward.

This is what the masters know: that a kiss on the cheek as you pass in the hallway is potent medicine. That looking up from that urgent work email to listen to a minor anecdote about what the baby did with his lunchtime sweet potatoes, in the end, matters more. That taking five minutes at the beginning of your day to connect over coffee far outweighs starting work five minutes earlier.

And so, this was our prescription for Alison and Jeremy. Their days were filled with back-to-back tasks: work, parenting . . . then more work and parenting. They were caught in the relentless cycle of life during a pandemic, with little relief and no real chunks of time to spend focused on each other. And the truth is, pandemic or no pandemic, life can get this way. Busy. Overwhelming. Nonstop. But as we told Alison and Jeremy: You don't need to magically make more time when there is none. No matter how frantic a day, there are always opportunities to turn toward. It costs very little in terms of time, and the payout is huge . . . *and* exponential. The more you do it, the more it works.

We asked them to find a few minutes at the start of the day for a check-in. They ended up doing it in the morning, in the fleeting few minutes before the kids came tumbling downstairs, wanting three different types of cereal. They'd lean on the kitchen island, standing up, with their elbows on the piles of remote-school paperwork and homework assignments, sipping their hot coffee, and ask each other: What's on your mind today? What are you looking forward to? What are you anxious about? They always ended up learning something important: a window into their partner's schedule and inner life. They always ended up laughing.

"Well, one thing I'm *not* looking forward to is that teacher who always makes us do animal noises." Jeremy sighed, and Alison cracked up—she hated it, too.

And then, throughout the day, we asked them to keep a lookout for bids for connection, and to turn toward them instead of letting them slip past. If Alison leaned over to murmur an observation about one of their kids while Jeremy was in the middle of an email, his assignment was to pause, take his hands off the keyboard, and give her his attention. The email would still be there in two minutes. The person who was waiting for it would never notice the difference. But Alison would.

Alison said, in one of our last Zooms: "Things are still hard. It's tough to balance both of our work schedules with the kids' remote school and everything else that has to get done. But I guess it just feels like we're on the same team again. It's us against the chaos, together."

You Have the Power

Turning toward is truly one of the most potent interventions we can recommend. Does it seem *too* simple and easy? Well, it might be simple, but it's not always easy to create a new habit. If this is already part of your relationship repertoire, *great*. Keep it up! This chapter, and the exercise that's coming up, can serve as a valuable reminder to keep turning toward a priority, not let it slip, and can give even more oomph to the micro-moments of positivity and connection you're already practicing.

If you feel like turning toward has faded from the culture of your relationship—don't worry. You can turn this around. Like turning a big ship, there can be a bit of a lag before the course correction you've done really starts to show up. But just turning the wheel a little bit, and then a little bit more, can really start to pay off if you keep it up. Think about how that big ship barely seems to shift direction at first, but the farther you go on that new course, the further you diverge from the old one—a widening V that takes you into entirely new territory.

Remember that study we mentioned earlier in this chapter, with the three groups that did the different workshop days? Well, there was one more group. In every study, there's a control group—that's typical. But we made a mistake with this control group.

While group 1 was doing the friendship day, group 2 the conflict day, and group 3 both, the control group didn't participate in any workshops at all. All they got was our book, *The Seven Principles for Making Marriage Work*, and access to seven hours with a licensed therapist by phone. Surprisingly, *none* of the couples in the control group ever accessed the therapist. They only used the book. And, surprise, surprise, they did remarkably well! By simply reading the book, they made significant positive changes to their relationships, and they *stayed* changed a year later when we circled back to them. While the most successful group was still the group that did both days of the workshop, the book readers came in a close second—they did better than any of the other remaining groups in the study. Their marriages improved, and stayed that way one year later—just from using a book together.

We think the real takeaway here is that if you want to improve the culture of your relationship for the better, with just a little reading, *you can do it*. Knowledge is power, and once you understand how much bids for connection, and how you each respond to them, can shape a relationship over time, the more you can make choices during a busy, time-pressured day that really align with your goals for your relationship over the long haul.

TODAY'S PRACTICE

THE TEN-MINUTE CHECK-IN

This is great to do at the beginning of the day, but you can do this at any time that works for you. The rules are simple—pick a time to check in with your partner when you have ten minutes to listen and not rush off anywhere. It can be in the morning, over coffee and before you start work, or in the evening after you've put the kids to bed. Ask them this simple question:

Is There Anything You Need from Me Today?
How does this create "turning toward"? First, it allows your partner to reflect on their own needs for a moment. Second, it makes clear that you really want to be there for them today if you can. And third, it gives hope that if they state what they need, you'll try to respond affirmatively.

It's just one sentence. But it does a lot. It's an invitation. It says *I love you and I want to be there for you.* It's a great trust builder. Trust, in a relationship, is a biggie. It's a complicated thing—but the foundations of it are basic. The principle behind trust is, "I've got your back, and you've got mine."

So when your partner responds to this question today, do everything in your power to say yes, and make it happen, whether it's "I need a break from the kids" or "I'd love to have lunch with you."

Extra Credit: Pick Up the Pennies

Today, think of every potential moment of connection—even the most fleeting—as possible money in the bank. Just as you would if you were walking down the street and saw dollar bills and coins scattered everywhere: *stop and pick them up*. It just takes a minute to bend down and grab it. So make it a point to do so—don't walk past any of them! Even pennies add up.

Be on the lookout for small bids for connection that you can engage with, turning toward your partner even just briefly. Keep an eye out for these, which are all invitations to connect:

- Eye contact
- A smile
- A sigh
- A direct ask for your help or attention
- Saying good morning or good night
- Asking for a favor
- Reading something aloud to you: "Hey, listen to this . . ."
- Pointing something out: "Look at that!"
- Calling your name from another room
- Seeming sad or down
- Physically carrying something heavy by themselves
- Seeming frustrated (with the kids, for example)

Every single moment you respond positively to your partner is money in your emotional bank account. And these deposits don't vanish—that positive balance will be there when you need it. With little moments throughout each day, you can make sure that your deposits outnumber your withdrawals.

Troubleshooting

What if you notice your partner make a bid for connection, but you really can't respond?

Of course, this will happen sometimes. Your emotional availability won't align neatly with your partner's emotional availability. And that's OK. So here's how to handle it.

- **When your partner makes a bid but you can't engage:** Say, "I'd really love to hear about this, but I have to _____ (send this email, get the kids to bed, and so on); can you remember to tell me about it later?" You acknowledge that you want to do the turning toward, but circumstances prevent it. Even if you're tired and don't want to engage, don't ignore the request. Just explaining, briefly, why you can't be available can go a long way.

- **When *you* make a bid and *they* don't respond:** If they miss a couple of your bids, just keep trying! But if it's a pattern, say to your partner: "I don't want to be critical, but I've been reaching out to you . . . what's happening for you right now that you haven't been responding?" It might be that they're busy, stressed, overwhelmed.

- **When a bid is made with negativity:** Some of the time, your partner's bid will sound negative or like they're picking a fight. (Example: "It wouldn't occur to you to make dinner tonight for once, would it?") Just ignore the negativity and respond to the deeper bid underneath. (You might respond: "I get that you're frustrated and tired. I'd be happy to make dinner and give you a break.") Wow—that's worth a lot in the emotional bank account.

DAY 2

ASK A BIG QUESTION

THINK BACK TO WHEN YOU FIRST MET YOUR PARTNER. REMEMBER WHAT it was like to have that fresh spark with them? To wait all day to see them, to feel like you were bursting with questions you wanted to ask? Everything from *What's your favorite movie?* to *If you could live anywhere, where would you live?* would roll effortlessly off your tongue as you performed that exhilarating dance of figuring out if this person was *the person*, the one you could see yourself with for a lifetime.

We had each moved to Seattle within two months of each other. John had just relocated to the West Coast after two decades of teaching in the Midwest; Julie was a Pacific Northwest native returning to her roots after two decades living everywhere else. Our paths crossed in a coffee shop we both frequented. Julie noticed John because he stuck out among the other patrons, looking smart and professorial. John noticed Julie's confidence and poise. He put down his empty cup and walked over to introduce himself, hoping to strike up a conversation. We started talking. And then we talked some more. And more, and more ...

The beginning of a relationship is exciting—there's so much to discover! The conversations you have are *full* of big, exciting, exploratory questions. It's effortless. We asked each other everything: *Where are you from and what brought you here? What do you do, and why did you choose it? What do you love to do when you're not working? What kind of music ... movies ... books do you like?* Drawn to each other, we were acutely aware of how much we didn't know about the other, and we wanted nothing more than to find out.

As a relationship develops, it can feel like watching a great new movie: You watch the plot unfold, both hopeful and nervous about all that might happen, as you find out more and more about this thrilling new main character in your life. You ask them about their childhood, about their hopes and dreams, their vision for the future. You discover which friendships are meaningful to them, or their favorite things to eat; you learn how they react when they're upset or excited. When we're in that heady, watershed time of first getting to know a romantic partner, we tend to talk *a lot*. We tell our stories and ask our partners theirs. Share our dreams for the future and ask them theirs. But over time as we get busy and the newness wears off, we stop asking about big things. We may start out with stuff like, *Do you see yourself having kids? If you could live anywhere, where would you live?* Then, eventually, other types of questions fill our conversations. *Did you take out the garbage?* or *Is it time to schedule the kids' doctor's appointments?* Questions like these take the place of heart-to-hearts. In part, this is simply practical—we do need to talk about who's going to do which tasks, what goes on the grocery list, how to manage finances together, and so on. But hectic as life is, we can't let all our questions for each other become about endless checklists.

Unlike movies, people change over time. That movie you watched with such curiosity and anticipation the first time around will unfold the same way the next time you queue it up. But people aren't like that. The same questions asked at different points in time will have different answers. Desires morph into new desires. Life goals shift. Bucket lists evolve. If we stop asking the big questions, while expecting our partner's answers to be identical to those we heard the last time we checked in, we might be in for quite a surprise.

Too Much Space

David and Gwen had been married twenty years when they first came to see us. In many ways, they had it all. David had a high-powered career he found fulfilling; they had three beautiful kids and a huge, gorgeous home; Gwen stayed home with the kids and threw herself into motherhood. They enjoyed financial stability—David worked long hours and pulled in a high salary, while Gwen had inherited wealth. So what was the problem? Why were they sitting in our office, on opposite sides of the couch?

The first thing they brought up was that since having kids, the romance had drained out of their lives. They never had sex anymore, and the physical distance and lack of sexual intimacy bothered them both. But we quickly discovered that sex wasn't the central issue—it was just a symptom of deeper problems. They hadn't really spoken to each other in years. Fifteen years earlier, when their first child was born, they turned their attention away from each other and onto the logistics of life and the immediate concerns of parenthood. The problem was that they never swiveled back toward each other. They asked each other, "Is this the right preschool?" "Did you call the plumber?" "Who's picking up the kids Friday?" They never asked, "Is this still the life you want?"

They might have been living in the same house, but there was too much space between them. In fact, their beautifully designed home was so big, they could walk from room to room and only rarely bump into each other. As a couple, you can live two parallel lives rather than a joint one together. And that's exactly what they were doing.

David and Gwen showed up in our offices because they didn't want to continue on like that, but they also didn't know how to create change. It seemed like any time they tried to connect, they were just too far apart. Everything was a fight or a missed connection, a failure to come together. So we had them begin again with a different category of question. The first step in rebuilding their marriage wasn't to ask each other "*How* are you?" but "*Who* are you?"

A Sheep Named Kevin

When the COVID-19 pandemic hit, Brianna and Tyler were living in a small two-bedroom apartment with their baby son. They'd had plans in the works to move to a bigger place across town, but now all that was on hold. The baby's day care closed and both of them shifted to working from home, trying to hit their full-time hours while swapping childcare duties. It was a lot. And yet their relationship stayed solid. They didn't turn on each other (even though they joked about being "animals in captivity"). There were plenty of stressors and issues they had to work through—like all couples, Brianna and Tyler had their own unique set of "unsolvable" problems. But through it all— even through conflict—there was an enduring sense of being on the same side.

What is their secret? Brianna and Tyler list various things they appreciate about the other: Tyler pulls his weight with childcare and handles the never-ending laundry. Brianna keeps their schedules well organized and is an innovative cook.

But mostly, this is what we notice: they are just so interested in each other.

Brianna shares her memory of one of the few times they got to go out on a date during the pandemic. After a two-week quarantine, they drove to Tyler's mother's house for a weekend. His mother watched the baby while they went out for a walk. It was snowing; they strolled through Tyler's old stomping grounds in rural Maine. Brianna had been there plenty of times before.

But this time, Tyler pointed out a particular field and started telling a story. He casually mentioned that "this is where Kevin, my sheep, lived."

"Excuse me," she replied. "We've been together *how* many years, and I'm just now finding out . . . that you owned a sheep? Named *Kevin*?"

They walked and talked for hours in the cold, until their fingers were numb and they had to turn back. The sheep named Kevin carried them back down a twisty road through time—they ended up talking about the lives they'd envisioned for themselves when they were teenagers, how their lives were exactly what they'd imagined in some ways, but also so, so different.

"Maybe it's silly, but I'll never forget that sheep named Kevin," Brianna said. "It's when I realized that he'll never stop surprising me."

Here's the thing: Anyone can surprise you if you give them the opportunity to do so. Brianna and Tyler have thrived, even through a pandemic lockdown, because they have never stopped being curious about each other.

Nice to Meet You . . . (Again!)

People change over the years, especially—as with David and Gwen—when one of them is mostly working and the other is raising kids. David and Gwen made a lot of progress just by shifting gears with the kinds of questions they were asking each other. We started them with ten minutes a day—that was about all they could manage! But it was enough to get them beginning to know each other again. They went back to the basics. They *met* each other all over again.

Any relationship is a process of meeting each other, again and again, over the years. You will change immensely over the course of your lifetime, and so will your partner. The cells in your body will shed and regenerate. The structures of your brain will change, radically. And as you go through life, new experiences will prompt you to recalibrate what you want, what you believe, how you see yourself. So take two people going through this chaotic, complicated life together, and they have many opportunities to miss big changes in themselves and in each other.

Humans are pack animals—we don't survive without connection to other people. And step one of connecting with someone else is knowing *who* someone is, and being known *by* them. And the number one way we find out who someone is—especially what is happening in their own internal world—is by asking questions. We do this naturally, even effortlessly, when we're dating. Then we get busy, we get involved in getting everything done by *being a team*. Being a team is great. But we have to remember that we're still two individuals, growing and changing and evolving over time.

In our work with couples, we talk about creating love maps. By "love map," we mean an intimate knowledge of your partner's inner world. Their hopes and dreams. Their beliefs; their fears; their desires. You have to ask questions not only to create love maps, but also to *update* love maps. And that means asking *open-ended questions*. That's what we mean by "big" questions: there's no yes/no reply that's possible; no quick drop-down menu of replies. An open-ended question doesn't have a predetermined answer. (We all know that the only correct answer to "Did you pay the electrical bill?" is "Yes, honey.") An open-ended question is full of possibility. There's not one road forward, but many—you don't know where the conversation will go next or where you'll both end up. And that's how you update love maps and make new ones—both by forging ahead into new territory and by looping back to previously mapped territory to see how it has changed. And we can't save these types of exploratory questions for date nights. They need to be a daily habit, not a "special occasion" thing.

For us, our own relationship has always been a rich, fertile ground for new theories about relationships—about what works to bring people together and the forces that drive them apart. Sometimes we figure something out with each other about how to navigate through a trouble spot, and we think, "Is this true for others? Would this hold up across a longitudinal study?" Our own fights and fixes would lead us back to the lab, where we could experimentally confirm (or disprove) what we'd noticed in our own relationship. Meanwhile, information would emerge from our lab studies that we'd try out ourselves. Our work with clients, our own relationship, the lab—each element of our lives has always informed the others, like a big circle, spiraling upward as we learn more and more about the inner workings of long-term love, how the gears work, what makes it work smoothly, and what gums it up.

One of the most powerful interventions that we created for the Gottman Institute came out of a fight that we had. It was ... a *really* bad fight.

Gaps in the Love Map

We'd been married for about four years. We were living in Seattle, running the Love Lab, seeing clients. We enjoyed our busy city life—we had our favorite cafés and restaurants; we took our daughter to parks and museums. But we liked to get out of the city. We started renting a place a few hours north, on one of the rugged, sparsely populated San Juan Islands, with its quiet little town, lush green forests, and endless hiking trails. We went up for a couple of weekends and enjoyed it so much that one summer, we rented a place on the water for a whole month. We went for long walks in the woods and canoe trips in the sea.

Both of us felt recharged by getting out into nature—but Julie especially so. When we arrived at the rental cabin, she could hardly wait to lace up her hiking boots and get out into the fragrant cedar forests, or hop into the canoe and dig her paddle into the fresh, silver water. John, meanwhile, agreed it was all beautiful, but he was just as happy sitting on the couch in front of the fire, toasty warm with a cup of coffee and a book on differential equations.

One day, arriving back home in the city after a weekend in the woods, Julie said, "I want to buy a cabin on the island."

John was startled. "Absolutely not," he said. "No way."

The argument flared like a match. "Why not?" Julie said.

"We can afford it!" She listed all the reasons they should go for it. John batted down each one—it wasn't practical. We couldn't afford it, not really. We went in circles. We started fighting so much about it, John asked around for a recommendation for a therapist to help. He found one he thought would be a good match—and after the initial consultation, he got the feeling she'd be on his side. (Side note: Not a good reason to pick a therapist!) We started talking things through with her, but we weren't getting very far—Julie could not understand why John wouldn't even consider something that was so important to her. John couldn't understand why Julie seemed so demanding and stubborn about this. We didn't *need* a cabin—the home life we had was working just fine.

One day the therapist said, "John, look. You don't have to cave in to Julie's demands. Tell her how it's going to be and she'll adapt."

John was horrified. He'd liked the idea of having someone in his court, but not if this was the solution—this kind of rigid, dogmatic, *my way or the highway* mentality. "Julie," he said as they left the office, "do I sound like that?"

Yes, she said, he did.

John still didn't want to buy a cabin, but he also didn't want to be that kind of oppositional person. And he didn't want to have that kind of marriage.

Back at home, instead of in the therapist's office, we finally started to really talk about it. We asked each other questions. *Why do you want this house so bad? Why are you so against getting this house?*

Julie described growing up in Portland, Oregon—an urban, populated city that also happened to have the largest wild municipal park in the country. The house where she'd lived with her parents was just blocks away, and she'd grown up in that park. She'd gone there to daydream, to run, to get away when things at home were tense—and they often were. When she just couldn't bear to be home, she'd sneak out the back door at night and sleep in the woods. She fell in love with trees. She felt more comfortable in the forest than around other people. To her, the rich, wet smell of soil and crushed evergreens was the smell of home, and safety.

Ever since she'd moved to Seattle, she'd been looking for that chunk of wilderness where she could feel that way again—and she'd found it, on the island.

John had grown up in Brooklyn. To him, nature was something to visit—*briefly*. You go on a picnic, put a blanket down, "and then wipe the nature off when you get home." But as they talked, he realized that his resistance ran much deeper than that. It had to do with his parents. They'd lived in Vienna, where his father was a rabbi and studying medicine. But they'd had to flee the Holocaust. They lost everything they'd owned—their apartment, furniture, clothes, photographs, and family heirlooms. They'd escaped by walking over the Alps into Switzerland with only a cube of sugar and a lemon in their pockets. When they later immigrated to the Dominican Republic, where John would be born, they arrived with nothing.

His dad used to say, "Don't ever think that where you're living is permanent. Nothing is permanent."

John's belief system was that you don't invest in belongings or property. You invest in education—which is something you can always carry with you, that nobody could ever take away.

After this conversation, nothing had changed about our finances, our likes and dislikes, our core personalities. But understanding each other better offered a way forward. In the end, we each got what we wanted by striking a compromise: John would support buying a little island cabin, if Julie agreed to keep a kosher kitchen in their house (which was important to John). And if he still felt the same way in two years, they'd sell it.

Spoiler alert: We didn't sell the cabin. This fight of ours took us on a new path—we now live on the island most of the year. But it *also* led us to a big idea that was a huge breakthrough in our work with couples. We call it the "dreams within conflict" exercise. It's the idea that most of our fights are not actually about what we *seem* to be fighting about, but something deeper, hidden beneath our positions on the conflict. When couples have a gridlocked problem where it's impossible to make progress or even talk about it, there's often an unrealized or even *unacknowledged* life dream, lurking below the surface. For us, we spent so much time fighting about whether or not we could afford the cabin that it was years before we finally got to the real question we each needed to answer: "What's your dream about this issue, and what's your nightmare?"

When we took the idea to the lab and into our couples workshops, we found that this approach to conflict (thinking and talking about each partner's dreams) created major breakthroughs

87 percent of the time—even with very distressed couples.[1] Some couples who came to the workshop were already divorced, but they were trying again. It even worked for many of them.

What did this tell us? That most conflict is not ultimately about personality, or about whose turn it is to do the dishes, or about how much money we have (or don't have) in the bank. It's about dreams, values, meaning, history, even *multigenerational* history. And this is why love maps matter. Why *questions* matter.

The more thorough your mapping of each other's inner landscape is, the more comprehensively you'll understand not only your partner's ideas about the future, but also their past and how it's shaped them. In our case, there were some big gaps in our love maps for each other. The more you fill those in, the more you will understand—quite literally—*where* your partner is coming from. We use that phrase all the time, but it's fascinating how perfectly it can describe knowing and being known by someone. You both had a whole life before you met each other. You come from your own unique "country"—filled with history and pain and joy, infinite detail and nuances—and your partner comes from another. When you seek to make a map of the "place" your partner comes from, you need to realize that this "mapping" will never be finished—it's a lifelong project of learning who your partner is and how they may change over time. And we'll promise you one thing: if you approach your partner with curiosity, you will never run out of new facts to discover. Even after a lifetime together, there will still be new stones to turn.

Be a Topographer, Make a Map

William and Marianne have lived on Orcas Island in Washington State for years. Like many people on the island, they moved up there to live a different kind of life—to live simply and sustainably, to use only what they needed, to make do with what they had. They don't have a lot, but they don't seem to mind—they grow much of their own food in their garden, and Marianne prides herself on fixing up broken equipment and furniture. The house they live in is one they built themselves. Their daily routines are familiar grooves worn from frequent use; they get along fine but sometimes worry that things are growing dull.

With the comfort and ease of mature love, we might miss the freshness and excitement of new love. We might think there isn't really anything new to explore about a partner. But the landscape within each of us, and within our partner, is always shifting and changing. And further, there is so much we might not have discovered, even after spending decades with someone. What happens when we start asking big questions again? *Surprises.*

William and Marianne had for years been working around their broken oven. It was one of those things she kept meaning to fix but just hadn't managed to. Besides, just using the stove top was working fine. They got along with that broken oven . . . *for fifteen years.*

Then came the COVID-19 pandemic, and like everyone, William and Marianne were marooned at home, looking for ways to fill the time. One day, Marianne asked William what he was interested in doing.

"One thing I'd really love to do is bake, and there's no way to bake," he said. "Couldn't we get the oven fixed? I really want to bake!"

Marianne was startled—William had never shown the slightest interest in baking in all these years. "Well," she said, "OK, if you really want to."

She put her "Ms. Fix It" pride aside and they called someone in to take a look at the oven. It turned out to be a really easy fix. And lo and behold, William was a *fabulous* baker. He immediately started churning out gorgeous loaves of bread, rye and sourdough, and all types of cakes, cookies, and muffins. It's been a complete delight. They work on baking projects together now, and William talks about how he learned to bake bread and why he loves it—all kinds of childhood memories emerged that Marianne had never heard before. He talked about how he'd always fantasized about opening a bakery someday.

It's been a wonderful activity for them—it has them spending time together, having fun, talking about the future again—and for all these years, she just had no idea.

This is your goal today, and for the rest of this week: Become a topographer. A love-map creator. Think of it as your job: You're going to go into this landscape that you think you know and *really* look around. What has changed? Where are the blind spots in your knowledge of your partner's inner world?

After thirty-four years of marriage, John is still doing this with Julie every day. He's always wondering: *What's on her mind right now? What does she have on her plate today? What's she worried about? What is she looking forward to? What's going on in our lives that's new (new friends, a new routine, the possibility of becoming grandparents) that I could check in about, to see what she's thinking about those things? What do I know about her right now, and what do I* not *know about her?*

In other words: *What am I missing?*

Often, when you start exploring, you find not only the information you were seeking, but something unexpected as well. The love map becomes a treasure map.

TODAY'S PRACTICE

ASK A "BIG" QUESTION

Today's assignment: Ask your partner one big question and see where it goes. A *big question* is an open-ended question; there's no dead end of a yes/no answer available. There is no one right answer—there are many—and your job as topographer is to follow your partner in whatever direction they go.

A big question doesn't have to be serious or momentous or tackle the meaning of life—although it can! Consider these:

- What are some unfulfilled things in your life?
- What legacy do you want our kids to take from your family?
- How have you changed in the past year?
- What are some of your life dreams right now?

A big question can also be fun, light, silly:

- If you could change into any animal for twenty-four hours, which one would you choose and why?
- If you could design the perfect house for us, what would it look like?
- If you could wake up tomorrow with three new skills, what would you pick?

Use one of these, or come up with one of your own. Just make it open-ended, and make it something fun to think about and discuss. You don't need to delve into your toughest topics or points of conflict today. You'll be surprised at where some of these questions will take you.

Here's one of our favorites, which is a great one whether you've just met or have been together for fifty years:

What Are Five Movies That You Feel Have Changed Your Life?

One couple we worked with started with this question— the husband posed it to his wife of two decades, and they never got past the first life-changing movie she thought of: *Singles*, the 1992 classic set in Seattle about a group of twentysomethings making music, working in coffee shops, launching their careers, falling messily in love. She described how watching the movie as a teenager imprinted the idea in her mind that she would, someday, be a twentysomething living in Seattle, working in a coffee shop. When she graduated from college, that's exactly what she did—and it was where she met her husband, who smiled at her and struck up a conversation over the screaming milk steamer as she made him a latte. The movie was responsible for their lives together—and she was shocked to discover that he'd never seen it. They watched it immediately, and spent the whole evening talking about the lives they'd each envisioned when they both first moved to the city years ago, how their joint life today was similar to that early vision, how it was different. They talked about the ways they'd both gradually gotten a bit off track from their dreams, and how they could get back on.

Ask a big question—and just see where it takes you.

Extra Credit: Keep the Conversation Going

Encourage your partner to say more. Make exploratory statements. Express interest and curiosity. You don't have to have a response to everything, and you don't have to solve their problems. In fact, try to resist problem-solving. That's a different kind of conversation and isn't the goal today. Making love maps is about listening, learning something new about the person you love, being surprised. If you feel the instinct to jump into problem-solving mode, or rebut something they're saying, just mentally set it aside. Tell yourself: *Not now—you can talk about that later.*

Easy ways to keep up the momentum:

- "Tell me more about . . ."
- "Tell me the story of that!"
- "How did you feel when that happened?"
- "Go on . . ."

Troubleshooting

You want to start asking your partner more big questions, and you want to *be asked* big questions by them. But maybe it seems hard or unfamiliar to start. Here are a few suggestions to consider if you have trouble getting the ball rolling:

- **Where are you in your relationship?** If you've just met, you don't want to ask something too personal. The person you're just getting to know may not be ready to jump into a conversation about their closely held life dreams and desires. Don't rush it—you're just starting to map each other's terrain. You'll keep filling in details as time goes on, especially if you make it a habit to always be wondering about your person, and trying to fill in the knowledge you lack.

- **How much time do you have?** The deeper the question, the longer you need to discuss it. You don't want to ask your partner about painful memories from childhood right before guests arrive for dinner. Pick a question that's proportionate to the moment. Over dinner is a great time, and you can broaden it to include kids or parents, or other family members and friends. "If you could magically have any skill or talent, what would you choose, and why?" appeals to ages four through one hundred.

- **Take a hike.** If you're feeling rusty at this style of communication (maybe it's been a while since you asked each other these kinds of questions), invite your partner on a walk. When you're not sitting there, staring at each other, but walking instead, you can shake off the dust and awkwardness! Somehow, moving your bodies helps oil the gears. And you can always take advantage of a small moment when you're doing something together—folding the laundry, cooking together, or cleaning out the garage.

- **Make it a game.** Download our free Gottman Card Decks app, which is full of virtual "card decks" full of questions and prompts inspired by the actual card decks we use in our workshops with couples. Find the deck called "Open Ended Questions." Take turns flipping through the cards and picking a question for the other to answer. Sometimes it's hard to find the perfect, natural, organic moment to ask a big question—instead, try the spontaneous "Let's play a game!"

- **Model it.** If your partner is slow to engage with the questions you pitch, offer information about yourself to soften the way. "If you could have a second career of any kind, what would you see yourself doing?" You answer it for yourself: "Since the pandemic, if I had it all to do over again, I'd be an epidemiologist. I'd love to do that instead. I used to be so interested in science, but I thought I wasn't good at it and never pursued it. I've been finding it fascinating, and what an amazing way to contribute. Anyway—what about you?" Show the way forward into the kind of conversation you want to have; it will make it easier for them to follow.

DAY 3

SAY THANK YOU

EVERY PARTNERSHIP IS UNIQUE, WITH ITS OWN UNIQUE CHALLENGES borne from each of our past histories, personalities, desires, communication styles, and more. On top of all that, the world puts its own pressures on us. Financial pressures. Work demands. Family demands. Discrimination. Every couple who walks through our door is an original, one-of-a-kind pairing, a mix of all of these factors and forces—there is no other relationship out there exactly like it. But at the same time, one of the incredible privileges of having worked with so many couples, across so many demographics, is being able to see the points of overlap where we are all the same. And one of the big points of overlap is this: We all want to be appreciated. To be acknowledged for our efforts. We all want to be *seen*.

You're Wearing Blinders

Noah and Melissa, a couple in their late thirties, had been successful in a lot of ways. Accomplished professionals, they excelled in their fields. For ten years, they'd been working hundred-hour weeks, launching and running their own company. They'd built a house together. Had a baby. The baby was now a toddler, and after a long wait, they were about to adopt another child. Wanting a change of lifestyle, they sold their company and the house they'd built; bought a new place, tried to slow down. But they were, as they described it, "on a treadmill of finding stuff to do." They launched themselves into renovating the new house; Melissa started writing a book. Things felt busy as ever.

They were ambitious, driven, smart, and hardworking—and they were exhausted. Ten years of overtime, of parenting, of every block of time being spoken for had left them burned out and overwhelmed. They had so much on their plate, it was spilling over. And they each felt they were shouldering the responsibility to tackle it all. When they looked around, all they saw was everything *not* done, everything the other one *wasn't* doing. The latest stack of bills unpaid; the electrical wiring for the new bathroom still unfinished; the endless lists of parenting tasks that someone had to do (the doctor appointments, new shoes, more diapers, and so on). They were immersed in the never-ending churn of work, life, and parenting, and the to-do list only seemed to get longer. They both felt like they were working as hard as they could and yet still losing ground. It was easy to look at the other and see (and then say) all the ways they were falling short.

Melissa had a matter-of-fact, analytical way of pointing out all of Noah's failures—he was supposed to have done *x* or *y*; he should have known to plan for *z*. To which Noah would respond explosively, getting angry and defensive. He felt wronged and maligned by her criticism, and lashed out. His reaction sparked more criticism from her—and the cycle continued, unbroken.

Noah and Melissa's situation isn't unusual. Couples are working so hard these days that they're on parallel tracks—like trains, they power along on their separate paths, never intersecting. We're each so caught up in planning what we have to get done, and then actually *getting* it done, that we don't often notice what the other person is doing. We have tunnel vision for our own tasks, challenges, our infinite to-do list—and it's a lot. We effectively have blinders on.

For a long time in the field of couples counseling, therapists assumed that unhappy couples were not being very nice to each other over the course of a typical day—in other words, not doing enough positive stuff like turning toward each other's bids for connection, helping each other out, making gestures of affection, and so on. They'd prescribe "positivity days" on which partners were tasked with increasing acts of kindness and service toward each other. Pretty quickly though, they tossed this tactic into the wastebasket—it didn't work. It turned out that, in general, people *were* being nice to each other—they just weren't noticing their partner doing it.

In 1980, two researchers, Elizabeth Robinson and Gail Price, ran a study in which they positioned two observers in people's homes, one to observe each spouse.[1] The mission of these observers was to objectively look for the positive things that people did for their partners. Meanwhile, they trained spouses to observe each other and record "pleasing and displeasing" behaviors on a spouse observation checklist.

What they found was amazing: Couples who were unhappily married missed 50 percent of the positive things the other partner did. It wasn't that the happily married couples were doing more sweet or helpful things for each other than the unhappily married ones—they were simply *better at seeing* their partner doing them.

When we observe our partners (and, in fact, when we observe our life in general), we have the tendency to notice the negative instead of the positive—the negative leaps out like a flashing neon sign. In part because of some evolutionary aspects of how the human brain works, we scan for problems by default, because solving them will help us survive. We also want to believe that we are objective observers of the world; that the information we gather is unbiased. Brain science tells us the opposite: When you're looking for problems, that's what you'll see. The attention and processing networks in your brain, which filter the world based on your assumptions and expectations, make sure of it.

Psychologist Robert Weiss coined the term "negative sentiment override" to describe what happens when negative feelings about a relationship become so strong and habitual that they negatively color the positive moments that are actually happening right before you.[2] When you're in the negative perspective, you see your partner and their actions through a distorted lens. You're not seeing clearly because you're not seeing the whole picture. You focus on the negative, miss the positive and even neutral events, and interactions become tinged with negative interpretations.

Consider whether the following examples sometimes describe you:

1. **You only see the things your partner has done wrong.** Imagine following your partner through the house all day, noticing, cataloging, and tracking every time your partner does something wrong or neglects to do something right. You don't let anything slide. You're building a list of all the ways your partner is falling short and failing you. You stop giving them the benefit of the doubt. When you see a pile of lunch dishes in the sink, you don't think, *Well, he had back-to-back Zoom meetings and was pressed for time.* You think, *He doesn't care about our home as much as I do.*

2. **You don't tell your partner what you need or wish for.** You feel that the things you need them to do are so obvious, you shouldn't have to point them out or ask. You think, *He knows this needs to get done and is just ignoring it,* or *She knows this is important to me and doesn't care.* And when they don't step up and perform the way you want them to, you blame them for not doing it.

3. **You do ask your partner for what you need or want, but when they don't do it in the same way you would, you criticize.** Your goal makes sense: for stuff to get done, and to get done right! You'd like him to do the laundry . . . but not shrink your sweaters. You'd like her to cook dinner once in a while . . . but not overcook the expensive lamb chops you bought. You give your partner a task that they are willing to

do for you . . . but then overcontrol how they do it. The end result isn't that they want to do it better next time; it just makes them not want to do it at all because they hate being controlled. And everybody ends up feeling resentful.

A thriving relationship requires a thriving *culture of appreciation* between partners, where we're as good at noticing all the things our partners are doing right as we are at noticing what they're doing wrong. It's easy to fall into the trap of only seeing what they're *not* doing. You develop a narrative where you're the one putting in all the effort, and you start to believe it's true. When you're only scanning for the negative, you'll easily find just that.

Disrupting this default mental habit means building a new one: scanning for the positive. If your culture of appreciation is waning or nonexistent, this is the most immediately effective tactic to jump-start its resurrection. Change your default setting and look for what's *right* instead of what's wrong.

Changing Your Filter

One couple we worked with was able to make a big change in this department, and it was all thanks to . . . *coffee.*

When Joel and David came in to see us, they were in a pattern of disappointing each other. Both felt they could never do enough to satisfy the other, no matter how hard they tried. Each reported a litany of complaints about the other—mostly small stuff, but we all know how that small stuff adds up like dishes in a sink, one dirty fork at a time. Both felt put upon, like he was doing everything. Both felt resentful.

One day they arrived for their session and seemed different. The shift in energy between them was palpable. There was a new warmth and closeness, and they even sat closer together on the couch. They seemed relaxed and more open than usual; the session was positive and productive.

We asked: What had changed?

They looked at each other. Joel smiled and shrugged. "He thanked me for making the coffee," he said.

The week before, Joel had gone away on business. It was his habit to get up early and make coffee. He'd leave it in the carafe, nice and hot, when he left for work, so when David (a major night owl) got up, there'd be a hot, fresh cup ready to go. Joel had done it for so long—since the early days of their relationship, before they were married—that it had become part of the background, something David had stopped noticing long ago. But when Joel was gone that week, David woke up to a silent kitchen and a cold, empty coffeepot. Grinding his own beans and fumbling around with the unfamiliar machine, he realized how much he appreciated and depended on that small, daily act of kindness. He started wondering what else he was taking for granted, what else he was missing.

Of course, one "thank-you" didn't magically fix everything. What it did do, though, was jostle their negative filters loose. David put it this way: "When I started looking for what he was doing right, it was just everywhere. Sure, there are still plenty of problems that pop up, but there are so many more positives, the problems just don't seem to make a dent anymore."

Scanning for the positive, instead of the negative, is a different way to use your brain—you have to train your brain to do this. Because you are, in many ways, preprogrammed to be on the lookout for the negative by default, this isn't quite as easy as flipping a switch and deciding to notice the positive. It'll take a little bit of effort at first—like learning to ride a bike. But here's a piece of good news: the human brain has incredible neuroplasticity, which means that you can "rewire" your neural circuitry by practicing looking for the positive.

Neuroscientist Richard Davidson, founder and director of the Center for Healthy Minds at the University of Wisconsin–Madison, discovered that positivity can actually be *seen* on a brain scan. The study used an electroencephalogram (EEG), which detects electrical activity in the brain through little electrodes attached to the scalp. When people are asked to describe their typical day during an EEG, those with depression have a lot more activity on the frontal right side of the brain than on the left, which is where we process fear, sadness, and disgust, among others—emotions that often cause us to withdraw from the world or avoid interactions with others. Meanwhile, the frontal left side of the brain is where we see the emotions that drive us to *approach* others and the world in general, like love, interest, curiosity, and even anger—anger is actually an "approach" emotion that gets you to engage with others, not withdraw. The *positive brain* and the *negative brain* not only look different on a brain scan, they also function differently—specific regions and pathways are electrically activated. When people are locked into scanning their world for the negative, it affects all of the brain's processing, shaping what you perceive, what you pay attention to, and how you feel—it's shaping your *experience of life*. It not only shapes how you see the world around you but also has "downstream effects," impacting your mental and even physical health.[3] Davidson found that mindfulness meditation—the practice of moving your attention back to the present moment whenever it wanders away—can reverse the negative habit of mind, first during meditation sessions and then, eventually, more permanently.[4]

The point is: When you're spending your time scanning for the *positive* instead of looking for the *negative* (for most of us, unfortunately, scanning for the negative is our brain's default mode of operation), you change your brain functionality at the cellular level. You create new pathways and activate new synapses. You train your brain to perceive the world differently, without that negative lens. It's good for your brain, your body, and your relationship.

The Power of the Positive Perspective

We ran a study on couples experiencing domestic violence to see if brain training for positivity, along with better ability to self-soothe, could make a difference for them. Now, a quick note: When we work with couples experiencing domestic violence, we're not talking about severe domestic violence with a victim/

perpetrator dynamic. We work on developing interventions for couples who experience mild to moderate domestic violence, where both partners can become violent during an escalated conflict, but no injuries are inflicted and both want to change. For this study, we developed a curriculum for people experiencing significant stress: couples who were in poverty and trapped in a cycle of getting violent during conflict.

To really *show* people what was happening in the brain and the body, we incorporated a small biofeedback device called the emWave (made by HeartMath) that measured heart rate variability and displayed colored "zones" to alert people to their mental and physical states. In the red zone, they were in a state of high arousal (not the good kind of arousal!), emotionally flooded, and prone to violent outbursts. But they could get to the green zone by slowing down their breathing, taking longer to exhale than inhale, and also *thinking about something positive* in their life that they felt affection or gratefulness around. The visualization of the positive was a powerful tactic to let go of stress, regulate the heart rate, and stay in the green zone.

The couples met two times a week with facilitators, using the biofeedback device for five minutes at a time while practicing the breathing and positive thinking exercises. By the end of the twenty-week study, and even a year and a half later, we saw diminished hostility, improved friendship, and greater passion and romance.[5] We had *eliminated* domestic violence and completely changed their physiology during conflict so that people could be calm even while disagreeing. The positive perspective is powerful—it significantly helped turn things around for extremely challenged couples, which means it can be a potent technique for us all.

Retrain Your Brain!

When we started working with Noah and Melissa, it was clear that they were in this kind of negative-filter mode. They were "red flagging" each other all day long. So the first thing we did was put a moratorium on criticism: It was henceforth banned! Zero critical comments were allowed. We put it to them this way: "Your brain is going to be finding negatives. Don't let the words that appear in your brain sift down and come out of your mouth. Just let them fall away unsaid, like sand."

The next step we asked them to take was to spy on each other. Watch the other person like a hawk all day and notice: *What are they doing right?* Just observe, without any intervention or commentary, and let's see what you find out.

Lo and behold, Melissa discovered that Noah was doing a ton of stuff for her and for their family and household. He gave the baby her bath every day, for one thing, and she noticed for the first time how much time and effort went into it, and how sweet he was with their daughter, how well he managed her. He was doing extra errands and housework so she could have more time to work on her book. She'd been feeling anxious about the book project and pressured, and he was giving her a lot of encouragement and emotional support. She was really stunned by how much he shouldered. She felt her own load lighten—even though her to-do list was still just as long. It felt different, knowing how much Noah was carrying, too.

When we helped her to recognize all the positive work he was doing, she started saying, "Thank you for doing that," all the time. It came to her naturally once she started seeing his efforts—she felt touched and grateful, and she said it out loud. And Noah? He absolutely *melted*. If he'd been all spikes and hard edges before, now he was a puddle of warm jelly. His defensiveness, combativeness, resentfulness—it all just fizzled away. Their negative downward spiral reversed right before our eyes—there was so much more warmth coming from her, it was easy for him to reciprocate and thank *her* for everything she was doing, even with the book project demanding so much of her time. The cycle of positive reinforcement and appreciation was like an updraft, carrying them higher and higher.

During the coronavirus epidemic, we saw many couples struggling with the negative filter. Mental health professionals reported a major spike in rates of depression. The constraints of pandemic life became a kind of crucible, putting us all under unusually high amounts of stress and pressure as external forces beyond our control kept us all home, cooped up with each other twenty-four hours a day. When you're suddenly together all day every day, you might be noticing a lot of ways that your partner does things differently than you would; their priorities are not in line with yours. Watching your partner walk past a pile of laundry to make themselves lunch when you've been cleaning up all morning can try the patience of a saint. But let's come back to the fundamental truth: at our core, we are *pack animals*. Pack animals do best when they try to cooperatively survive under stress, rather than crumble into an "every man for themselves" mentality. The more we can interact in a positive way—even if it feels like a stretch at times—the easier it will be to get through, and even flourish, amid challenging times. Looking for what your partner is doing right is a small mental adjustment that will, over time, not only change the processing patterns of your brain, but will also become a powerful antidote to the relationship breakers we call the "Four Horsemen of the Apocalypse." These come galloping in when we don't build a strong culture of appreciation: criticism, contempt, defensiveness, and stonewalling.

What we can do to drive out the Four Horsemen—or stop them from ever getting in in the first place—is *to make the invisible visible*. We find the good that's been hidden and overlooked, notice it, and appreciate it. And further, we can turn our lens on ourselves. Ask yourself: When you feel affectionate toward your partner, or grateful for them, do you express it? Do you communicate it? Or are you assuming that they somehow already know?

Instead of keeping those thoughts and feelings silent, we're going to work on establishing a new habit of saying them out loud. If you feel it, *say it*. When you introduce this habit, it's incredible how quickly the dynamic between you and your partner can heal or improve. A couple we worked with recently, Tony and Sunny, was in a particularly challenging situation: the husband, Tony, was co-parenting his daughter with his ex-wife, Jennifer. Tony's relationship with his ex-wife had become, unfortunately, very toxic. The nuances of co-parenting had become difficult to navigate; stress was high, and Tony and Sunny found themselves constantly fighting over how to handle every interaction or issue with Jennifer. It felt to them like they were being targeted and attacked from the outside by Jennifer, like she was intentionally injecting stress and trauma into their marriage. But, in reality, Tony and Sunny were so focused on stress and crisis that they were also focusing on everything negative that the other one was doing, and that magnified their stress. They weren't being affectionate. They weren't seeing the positive. They were constantly criticizing each other, too. When Tony had an issue with Jennifer, he now felt he couldn't bring it up with Sunny because she'd twist it and hear it as an attack on her. The negative filter was so pervasive that by the time we saw Tony and Sunny, their attitude was, "Why are we even in a relationship? What's the point?"

Our intervention? *Change the focus.* Accept that there's going to be stress and difficulty from Jennifer. There's nothing you can do about that. Instead, focus on making a space inside the home and the marriage healthy and supportive for each other. We gave them each a mission. Tony's goal was to make Sunny's week positive. Sunny's was to focus on appreciating Tony's efforts.

When they shifted the focus, they were suddenly able to see how wonderful their partner was, and how much they were each doing. They were able to problem solve together, and to manage Jennifer and co-parenting without letting that toxicity creep into their own relationship and drive a wedge between them. It was actually quite amazing. In our actual sessions, we were only able to minimally help Tony and Sunny. They did it themselves, at home, by really employing this strategy of appreciation. They became highly skilled at shielding their relationship from that barrage of negativity. They'd made it bulletproof.

TODAY'S PRACTICE

SAY THANK YOU!

Saying thank you is one of the first things we're taught as children—to show appreciation and gratitude when someone does something kind, or goes out of their way, for us. You probably say it automatically, almost without thinking, all day long: to your work colleagues, the bagger at the supermarket, the stranger who holds the door for you. But in our most intimate relationships, we can forget how important saying thank you really is.

Our partners want to know that they've pleased us. That their efforts—however imperfect they can sometimes be—are still seen and appreciated. That they aren't taken for granted or invisible. For David and Joel, saying thank you broke the ice and opened up a new path forward. Melissa and Noah found that when one person started the cycle of appreciation, it was so easy for the other to join in and strengthen it. Here's your assignment for today:

Step One: Be an anthropologist.

For the rest of the day (or tomorrow, if you're reading this at night), your job is to *be a spy*. Forget your to-do list. Take a few hours off work. (Or call in sick—we'll sign the doctor's note!) If that's not possible, carve out whatever time you can to be around your partner as they're going about their day. To train your mind to do this, you need to—for a short time anyway—eliminate all other distractions, and just watch.

Keep a close eye on your partner today, whenever you can. Follow them around. Write down everything your partner does, especially the positive stuff! Don't write down the negatives, such as ignoring a pile of papers you asked them to pick up. Instead, note that they worked hard all morning with intense focus and got a lot done, or that they cleaned up the breakfast dishes, fielded phone calls, picked up the toys strewn all over the living room, made you a coffee when they went to make one for themselves. Notice the steps in some of the tasks that have been their department for so long, because you might not know what's involved. For example, one couple we worked with tried this exercise, and the spouse who was "playing anthropologist" for the day was shocked by how many steps went into getting their son ready for school: waking him up; getting him dressed; convincing him to get his shoes on; tying his shoes; and packing his backpack, his lunch, his warm jacket and mittens. He hadn't realized the job was as demanding as it was, and he had a new appreciation for his wife's efforts every morning.

You don't have to hide the fact that you're spying—this doesn't have to be Mission: Impossible. You can tell your partner you're observing them to get a better sense of their day, and everything they do. Their behavior isn't going to change much just by knowing you're watching. If you're doing this together, take turns—you be the observer for a while, then switch roles. Look for the things you might not be able to see easily, because of conflicting schedules or distractions. Use X-ray vision to see everything your partner does, no matter how small and routine. And as you watch, go beyond the basics of tasks and errands. Observe how your partner conveys affection when they interact with the kids and others. The to-do lists of life are long and never-ending, and they automatically replenish themselves every day. There will always be something more to do; something not done. Is your partner spending time interacting with your children, talking on the phone with aging parents, supporting colleagues, connecting with friends? Notice how your partner shows kindness, generosity, and encouragement, and the ways that they invest in relationships. This is time well spent.

Step Two: Say thank you.

Say thank you for something routine. If you've been observing your partner closely, you'll have a lot of opportunities to do so. Thank them for something they're doing right, even if it's small, even if they do it every day—in fact, *especially* if it's small and they do it every day! But don't just say "Hey, thanks." Tell them why this small thing is a big deal to you. "Thank you for making the coffee every morning. I love waking up to the smell of coffee and the sounds of you puttering away in the kitchen. It just makes me start the day off right."

Gratitude: it's good for your health, and good for your relationship. With one thank-you, you begin to build (or continue to strengthen) your culture of appreciation. It's one of the top skills employed by the masters of love and longevity.

Troubleshooting

If you're crunched for time . . .

If you can't play hooky from work, or carve out a few hours, don't worry—you can still gather some good data on your partner using other tactics.

Trade roles. If you're always the one who gets the kids off to school, have your partner do it today instead. If he or she is always the one to make dinner, you do it tonight. You two might even make a quick list of everything you each do, then pick a couple of things to flip-flop on. See what it feels like to put yourself in each other's shoes.

Observe each other during mealtime. Mealtimes are a good touch point during the day to observe each other. Notice what your partner does before, during, and after mealtime, whether it's prep, cleanup, or other tasks involving the house, kids, bills, and so on. John always notices how much Julie packs into her post-breakfast time before work—while he's finishing his breakfast, she's sweeping the deck, watering the plants, filling the bird feeder. Any meal that you share together during a busy day can be a good, concentrated time to "spy" on your partner.

If you're having trouble getting out of the negative perspective . . .

Take a look at your past. Sometimes, when people have had crappy caretakers, they'll merge together what their caretaker did and what their partner is doing now. Without meaning to, they'll superimpose these feelings onto their partner—it's like the ghost of this parent or caretaker is there, getting in the way.

What to do about it? Try to separate out the negative feelings about that past relationship by being in the *here and now*. Try to notice if you're mentally traveling back in time, making assumptions and resurrecting old feelings. We mentioned mindfulness meditation as a way to change the brain—this can help here. Focus on this specific moment, this specific person, what you can tangibly observe. Ask yourself: *Have I had these negative feelings before this relationship ever began? Who with? What set off those feelings?* Identifying, naming, and sourcing these types of negative thoughts and feelings can help you let them go.

If it feels like you're seeing the positive, but your partner is not . . .

Remember: You're changing you own mind and mental habits when you do this. You're not changing your partner. Ultimately, how they think and feel is not in your control. But changing your own way of looking at the world is powerful. You're disrupting the cycle of negativity—you're refusing to feed it or give it any fuel to continue—and that is so important.

If you still have pervasive negative feelings . . .

You might be dealing with depression. People who are depressed have a brain-generated mountain of negative thoughts and feelings, not only about themselves but also about others. It's extremely hard for them to reach up and grasp their positive thoughts and feelings about their world and the people in it. If you're really having trouble finding your positive perspective, or you notice your partner is struggling to do so, the real struggle may be with depression.

Depression can be helped by medication and effective psychotherapy. If you think depression is the "third party" in your relationship, seek professional advice from your family doctor, who may refer you to a psychiatrist or psychotherapist especially trained to help you. And don't worry, you won't be alone. Recent data indicates that at least 9.5 percent of Americans regularly experience some degree of depression;[6] however, during the COVID-19 pandemic that number tripled, rocketing up to 32.8 percent.[7] And after all, if you are struggling with depression, why should you just continue to suffer when good help is available? Professional assistance can help both you and your relationship. You won't be sorry you reached out.

DAY 4

GIVE A REAL COMPLIMENT

MOLLY AND CAROLINE MET IN THE MOUNTAINS. THEY WERE FRESH OUT of college, young and ready for adventure. They'd each applied to AmeriCorps and had ended up working for the US Forest Service on the same trail crew. Hiking into the North Cascades in Washington State, they would haul heavy tools for clearing fallen trees and rebuilding trails, and would even sleep out under the stars when it was clear. One day on the trail, Molly and Caroline ended up working side by side and fell into conversation. It was a hard day of work, but the hours dissolved as they talked about movies they'd both loved, places they'd traveled, places they wanted to go, their pasts and their imagined futures. It was one of those conversations that started light and fun but got deep *fast*.

Fast-forward ten years: Molly and Caroline are married. They don't work in the mountains anymore, lacing up hiking boots and hauling chain saws—they've settled into careers in environmental activism. It doesn't pay much, and the setbacks can be crushing, but they both love what they do. A few years ago, they managed to buy a house in north Seattle, a lovely little Craftsman in a tight-knit, walkable neighborhood that's close enough to downtown that they can bike to work, and close enough to the mountains that they can drive out for a hike on the weekends at the drop of a hat. They turned their small square of front lawn into an efficient little garden, building raised beds out of cedar planks. But the city has been growing more and more expensive, and financial pressures weigh heavily on them. They don't travel as much as they once thought they would—in fact, barely at all. They've been talking about starting a family, but the costs associated with it are scarily high. Molly thinks they should leave the city and move out to someplace cheaper and wilder; they can find new jobs and embark upon a whole new adventure! But Caroline likes their house, their garden, their life. She likes her job. She likes things as they are.

When we started working with them, they were locked in a feedback loop of resentment and defensiveness, each staking out her own territory and deflecting what she saw as an attack on her own needs and desires. And *everything* felt like an attack. It was impossible for either of them to bring up a topic for discussion without the conversation immediately devolving into a micro-war. When Molly brought up having a baby during one of our sessions, Caroline immediately tensed.

"I think you're just restless," she said. "You always want to just get to the next thing. Why can't you just sit still? Why can't what we have be good enough for you?"

"This is what we talked about, Caroline. We always said we would have kids when the time was right. We're going to miss our chance. You can't drag your feet on everything and expect me to wait around for you."

They were starting to lob the kinds of criticisms that can corrode a relationship—the kind that eat through fondness and friendship like rust through metal. But they were in our office for a reason: They wanted to fight for the relationship. They wanted to find a way forward. They'd fallen in love working side by side, blazing trails into the wilderness, but now they couldn't forge even the thinnest path together.

We asked them a question that is one of the clearest litmus tests of any relationship: "Tell us how you met."

And they did. They each told versions of their story, which they remembered vividly. We heard about uncomfortable nights on the rocky ground, holding hands secretly in the dark from two separate sleeping bags. Even in the midst of their ongoing conflict, they easily answered the question: "Why did you fall in love with her?"

Caroline: "She was so bold and adventurous. She was always at the front of the group, leading us to the next job, tackling the hardest tasks. She seemed up for anything."

Molly: "She really listened when I talked. She was so thoughtful. She was always so patient and steady—it was like landing on solid ground after being at sea."

It was easy to see that within their current struggles, there were qualities that they deeply appreciated and admired about the other. And they were able to access those feelings of fondness and admiration—it was right at the tips of their tongues. They were going through a tough time with some big decisions looming, but we already knew they were going to be OK.

It wasn't just a hunch: Data from the three thousand couples we followed, some for as long as two decades, in the Love Lab showed that couples who stay happily together are easily able to name specific qualities they love and appreciate about their partner. They have vivid memories of their past together. When they describe that shared history, their narrative is an overwhelmingly positive one—they emphasize the good times and the upsides.[1]

There will always be conflict in any relationship, no matter how solid the partnership, no matter how deep the intimacy. We now know that the majority of problems couples face are *perpetual* problems—they are not solvable. They can't be fixed. But couples who take the time every day to notice and hold in mind what they admire about the person they've chosen to weather the slings and arrows of life with are the ones who succeed long term. Admiration isn't something that just happens—it's something you *do*. Actively admiring the other person—appreciating them not just for what they do, but for *who they are*—is like air in a life raft: you float above the waves, even when they get rough.

Why Did You Fall in Love with Your Partner?

Think back to the beginning, whether it was months ago, years ago, or decades ago. Recall the moment you met. The moment you thought, *I want to get to know this person better.* The moment you decided that you wanted to be together long term and make a life together. What were the qualities that drew you to them initially? What excited you about this person? What did you admire about them? When you pictured a life with them, what was it that you valued in them? Who were they to you?

We could fill a book with the origin stories we've heard over the years: *It was the sound of her laugh from across the room, cutting through the crowded party—her joy was contagious.*

It was the way he talked to children, before we had any of our own—I knew I wanted to be a parent with him.

She was so authentic and unafraid to be herself. She obviously didn't care what anybody else thought.

He was so fun to talk to. We talked so long on our first date, they had to kick us out of the restaurant.

Now, if we were to ask these same people about their partner's flaws, they'd surely be able to come up with a laundry list of grievances (in fact, many of the above comments came from people who were, like Molly and Caroline, in our office because they were having a really tough time). Nobody's perfect. Each of us is our own unique bundle of good qualities and . . . well, not so good qualities. It's what makes us human. And frankly, it's what makes us lovable—we love each other *because* of our idiosyncrasies, not in spite of them. But when you're living together, raising children together, maybe even working together (as we've been doing for the past thirty-three years!), and trying to keep afloat in the messy chaos of life, it can be hard to remember that. Someone's habit of forgetting to move the laundry to the dryer before it mildews, or their inability to notice that the bathroom is falling into a state of horrifying disrepair, can start to seem not so lovable at all.

As we talked about in the last chapter, when we start looking at each other through a negative lens, we can find a *lot* to be critical about. And that negative perspective doesn't stop with what your partner is *doing* right or wrong. It can infect how you think about them as a person. *He never cleans the car* becomes *he's lazy and sloppy. She avoids my mother* becomes *she's antisocial and judgmental.* This way of thinking about each other leaves the door wide open to those relationship killers, the Four Horsemen: criticism, defensiveness, stonewalling, and, perhaps most destructive of all, *contempt.* Contempt, which emerges from a pattern of negative thinking and criticism of your partner, is deadly poison for a relationship. It's the number one predictor of divorce.[2] It impacts the mental health of both partners.[3] And it can literally make you sick: studies found that partners who heard their partner's contempt for them were significantly more likely to catch colds, flus, and other infectious illnesses in the coming year.[4]

The good news? There's an antidote for this. We have more control over how we see each other than we might think, even through tough times, stress, setbacks, disagreements, or periods of disconnect. Like scanning for the positive instead of for the negative (as we discussed in the last chapter), this is a habit of mind that we can cultivate simply by practicing it, in small ways, every day.

The masters of love don't have fewer flaws than the rest of us. They don't sail through life without ever running into challenges or conflict, never getting annoyed with how their partner chews or never getting frustrated that their partner isn't better at managing money. They have just as many foibles and imperfections as the rest of us. But what they're *great* at is seeing their partner's innate good qualities. They are highly skilled at holding—in the front of their minds—what they admire about their chosen person. And that becomes impenetrable armor against the forces that break down a relationship.

The Math Equation That Makes You or Breaks You

Here's a statistic from the Love Lab that everybody needs to know: *five to one*.

That's the ratio of positive to negative interactions *during a conflict* that you need to have in order to keep love alive over time. For every one single negative interaction, you'll need five positive ones to make up for it.

We discovered this in one of our first big longitudinal studies in the Love Lab: When couples came in, we sat them down, made them comfortable, and then gave them fifteen minutes to resolve a disagreement while we sat back and watched. Later, we pored over their recordings and transcripts and logged every little moment, categorizing each one—a smile, a little joke, touching the other person's hand, expressing empathy and interest, saying "I understand," nodding their heads, being kind: these were all *positive*. A nasty remark, raising their voices, snapping, criticizing, blaming, acting disinterested: these were *negative*.

We watched the couples, logged the data, then released them

back into the wild. Six years later, we followed up. And lo and behold: it was the couples who had maintained at *least* a five-to-one ratio (or more!) during conflict who were still happily together, still feeling the love.[5]

Negativity will happen during conflict. These couples weren't perfect. And that's OK—we're all only human. We all make mistakes and take stuff out on our nearest and dearest. We can be unfair. We lose perspective. We get caught up in the heat of the moment. We say something we don't mean, or in a way we wish we hadn't. And we don't need to be emotionless or polite, or avoid tough conversations. But we do need to check on our positivity meter, to make sure it's accumulating enough positives. Negativity can be a potent poison. Negativity has much more power to inflict damage and cause pain than positivity does to heal and bring you closer. That's why we need *five times* more positives than negatives during conflict. But know this: you *can* win the war against negativity. You can "fill up your glass" with positive interactions so that when there *is* a drop of negativity, it's diluted. It loses its potency.

Now, a critical caveat—we've been talking about the minimum ratio of positive to negative interactions *during conflict*. What about the rest of the time?

That ratio jumps . . . to *twenty to one*.

In your typical, everyday life, as you and your partner are going about your business—cooking meals, negotiating chores, parenting your kids, chatting about your day—you'll need, at a minimum, *twenty* positive interactions for each negative one. The masters of love maintained that twenty-to-one ratio, and more. The couples who were headed for divorce or unhappiness showed a skewed ratio, with that number ticking up on the negativity side.[6]

So why does this happen? Well, often, we aren't even aware of our negative impact on our partners.

Does Your *Intent* Match Your *Impact*?

One of the first ways that we "coded" interactions between couples, in order to find behavior patterns to compare unhappy couples with happy ones, was through a device called "the talk table." John and Robert Levenson (John's first research partner) built it early on, before we launched the Love Lab in Seattle, when they were just starting out in their work looking for mathematical patterns in the love lives of human beings. It was a funny-looking table, angled on both sides and with buttons on each side, like a video game you were going to play with your partner. If you were to come into that first lab of ours with your partner as a participant, here's how it would have gone down: You'd sit down at the table, one of you on each side, and we'd get you talking. We'd ask you a question such as: *What's one of your biggest areas of continuing disagreement?* We'd prompt you to work on resolving it . . . and then watch.

You'd be alone in the room, but we'd be observing from an adjacent one—cameras trained close on your faces would capture your every fleeting expression, while we watched on a split-screen TV.

In front of each of you there'd be two rows of buttons: one row was for *intent*, the other row was for *impact*. There were five buttons to a row, ranging from positive to negative, with neutral in the middle—picture one of those survey quizzes you have to take online about your experience shopping somewhere. The buttons range from poor to great with a few options in between. You'd take turns speaking with a light glowing on your side of the table when it was your turn; when you were done, you'd flip a switch to give your partner the floor. Each time you handed off the baton, each of you would record your experience of that small portion of the conversation. If you'd just been speaking, you'd press the button on the intent row that corresponded with how you intended to come across to your partner. Meanwhile, your partner would press the button on the impact row that best described how he or she felt in response to your comment. We wanted to know: Do people have the impact they intend to have?

When we recruited couples for this experiment, we wanted to make sure we could get a really good comparison between the habits of happy couples and unhappy ones. We wanted to be able to really say something about *great* relationships and how they stood apart from the crowd. So we oversampled from the extreme ends of the spectrum: we recruited couples who were either really happy or really unhappy—nothing in between to muddy the data.

We were looking for a couple of things: Was there a mismatch between *intention* and *impact*? Did people actually have the effect on each other that they intended to have?

Here's what we found: intentions made no difference! Everybody had positive intentions, even if their behavior was angry and hostile. Intention meant nothing; impact was everything. And the difference between the extremely unhappy couples and the very happy couples boiled down to one simple thing: the happy couples were kinder when they spoke to each other—they treated each other more gently, without criticism, contempt, or sarcasm. And there was a *dose-response relationship*, meaning the kinder they were to each other, the better the outcome.

Now, there was not just one profile of the kind of couple who would turn out to be happy and stay together for the long haul. Tolstoy wrote, "All happy families are alike, but every unhappy family is unhappy in its own way." Unfortunately for Tolstoy, that turns out not to be scientifically true. Some successful couples were quite emotional; others not emotional at all. Some people were highly expressive, even volatile; others were like the poker-faced, severe couple from the famous painting *American Gothic*. The one thing that did not change at all was that ratio of positive to negative interactions. The happy couples were more positive, more empathetic. Again, everybody had positive *intentions*—but for happy couples, impact matched intention.[7]

We ran it again, this time with a different demographic: the first study had had college and grad students as participants, so the next time, we went out into a rural community in Southern Indiana. But even so, the results were essentially the same—the margin of error was only in the second decimal place.[8] It's a pretty stunning result, to get such a stable finding. And we were able to use these findings to observe couples and predict if they'd be happy together or not.

So we know that we need to meet this certain threshold of positive interactions. And we know that our positive intentions don't always land. So what do we do?

Cultivate Compassion

In the previous chapter, we talked about the damage that ensues if you look around and see only what's wrong, incomplete, imperfect. Now, take that negative lens and consider how often you apply it to your partner—not just what they do (or don't do), but *who they are.*

Yesterday, we were focusing on gratitude, and saying thank you for specific actions. What we want to talk about here is *admiration.* Admiration is about fundamentally admiring and valuing who your partner is, not necessarily what they do. They may demonstrate who they are through their actions, sure, but admiration links back to their personality, their innate qualities—from the superficial (their gorgeous eyes!) all the way down to the deep and profound (their spirituality, their optimism, their capacity for love).

We want to make a really important point here: this is *not* about putting on "rose-colored glasses." It's a common phrase, but we never use it. It implies a sort of false or deceptive positive spin, and that's not at all what we're talking about. We're talking about seeing your partner fully: leaning into their wonderful qualities as well as having compassion for their *enduring vulnerabilities.* This is a term coined by Thomas Bradbury, a researcher and psychologist at UCLA, to describe the particular sensitivities we develop over time because of our life experiences, all the way back to childhood. Our enduring vulnerabilities are often the root cause of those qualities that our partners might not love so much about us (like insecurity, fear, quickness to anger, or tuning out when we should be tuning in), but we can live together so much better when we understand their origin.

When we were first married, we had a fight that seemed to blow up out of nowhere. John was driving home from work one day and a worry popped into his head: *Did we ever pay that plumber?* It's important to him that we promptly pay the tradespeople we hire—he knows people depend on that income and he wants to be on top of it. But maybe Julie had mailed the check. He walked in, set his coat and bag down, and said, "Hey, did you pay the plumber?"

The anger on her face shocked him. "Did YOU pay the plumber?" She stormed out.

John was baffled. He remembers thinking, *Did I marry a lunatic?* Her reaction seemed so out of proportion to events. They hadn't been married long, but if he knew one thing for sure, it was not to stew on it, and instead just go and talk to her. When they talked, Julie described coming home from school as a child, and how when she walked in the door, her mother would always first say something critical before saying hello: "Is *that* what you wore to school?" "Where's your purse? Did you forget it *again*?"

Julie told John: "When we haven't seen each other all day, it's important to me that you at least say hello first, that you say something kind, or maybe ask how my day went."

Once he understood, it was an easy fix to make.

Now, the first time John sees Julie after they've been apart, he shows that he's really glad to see her—that he's glad she exists.

Admiring and appreciating your partner isn't just about seeing the good stuff. (That's great too, and it's what we'll be doing in the exercise shortly.) It's also about understanding the negative things they live with. What we see in happy, thriving relationships is that people do genuinely admire each other for all the wonderful qualities they each possess, and when it comes to the inevitable not-so-wonderful qualities, they're able to have compassion for each other's enduring vulnerabilities.

Some people have had really tough stuff happen that has left them with vulnerabilities and fears that make it difficult to live with them sometimes. But those of us who are partnered with people who have this kind of backstory need to remember that these people we love are survivors. They've had to summon up a lot of courage at certain points in their life to keep on going. And maybe they are sometimes irritable, anxious, or fearful. But they survived what they went through, and that may have scarred them.

When you look at your partner today, and every day, you can focus on their flaws, or you can focus on the qualities that make them indispensable to you, wonderful to you, attractive to you. It's a choice. It's an *active* thing you do to fan the flames of long-term love. If you've ever lit a fire, you know exactly what we mean—just like a fire, a relationship needs tending. You don't just leave it alone and hope for the best. You tend it. You add scraps of kindling. You give it a breath of air.

That's what admiration is—an *action* we do. That we need to remind ourselves to do it doesn't cheapen it or make it any less genuine. This is how the masters of love do it. To be in love for the long haul is to *choose* to see the best parts of our partners first, instead of looking for the worst.

If this has been lacking in your relationship, one strategy is to come back to that question we asked you at the beginning of this chapter: *Why did you fall in love with your partner?* Reflecting on this question can be an amazing way to reset and regain some perspective. Reaching into your shared past and pulling up fun memories, adventurous memories, memories of connection, sexy memories—this can regenerate your innate capacity to visualize all the good in your relationship, instead of letting the good remain invisible or buried under the minutiae of daily life.

But here's the thing: If you don't do this consistently, the past might not be there for you when you reach back for it. When things start to go sour—when admiration fades and people forget why they like and love each other; when the negative perspective sets in—even our memories can become corrupted, like a virus in a computer file. *Contempt* sets in, which is a relationship destroyer. It will infect the foundational "code" of your relationship. What we see with the relationships that (sadly) aren't actually salvageable is that even when these partners reach back into the past, they can no longer remember the things they once loved and admired about each other.

That's why *small things often* is our prescription—because a daily micro-habit of reminding yourself of one specific reason you love and admire your partner will take you miles in terms of a lifetime of love. Part of admiration is *cherishing* what you have with this person, amplifying their positive qualities in your mind and minimizing the negative ones. It's something you can do any time, even for a few minutes. Reflecting on what you cherish about your partner, and why no one on the planet could ever really replace them, is incredibly powerful. And you can double the impact of this powerful act by sharing with your partner what you cherish about them.

The capacity to admire your partner is like bulletproof armor for a relationship. Contempt is corrosive—if it gets in there, it can rapidly eat through all the good in a marriage or partnership like rust does to metal, no matter how strong and ironclad it once was. Admiration is a powerful protectant ensuring that contempt never even gets a toehold.

The Positive Perspective: The Most Potent Antidote There Is

It's quantifiable: You need roughly twenty times as much everyday positivity as there is negativity between you and your partner. An amazing way to create positivity is to admire your partner, and then say it out loud. In a jam-packed day, it's possible to just let the real stuff of life slip away—so take a few moments to regard this human you're going through life with and remember, *Oh yeah, I really love the way she comes home every day so jazzed to tell me about her work.* Don't let those thoughts and feelings pass without sharing them with your partner. Grab on to them; hand them to your partner like a tiny gift. It's a gift for you, too.

Affection, respect, and friendship are the foundation of everything else in a marriage or any long-term relationship, from how fiery your sex life is to how you can effectively navigate a thorny discussion about finances. But it doesn't "just happen." It comes from intention. From action. From choice. You choose, every day, to perform these small actions that fill up your emotional bank account. You make time to check in. You stay curious: *What don't I know about her? What's his day been like?* You keep a lookout for bids for connection and you turn toward whenever you can, because now you know that even the most fleeting of engagements—a smile, an encouraging phrase, a follow-up question that communicates *I'm listening; I care about what you're saying*—are all money in the bank. You retrain that squirrelly human brain of yours to scan for the positive instead of the negative, reprogramming your neurons to notice what's *right* instead of what's *wrong*, which has trickle-down effects throughout your brain, body, relationship, and experience of life. And you make it a top priority to hold in the front of your mind the things you love and admire about your partner. Not just the things they *do* for you, but *who they are* fundamentally.

TODAY'S PRACTICE

GIVE YOUR PARTNER A GENUINE COMPLIMENT

Today's action is essential whether you have a thriving culture of admiration between you and your partner or whether your relationship needs some serious rehabilitation. If this is an area of strength for you, *wonderful*. Let's keep that fire well fed.

For some couples (and if this includes you, you aren't alone), fondness and admiration seem like distant memories. That doesn't mean they aren't still there, waiting to be called back to life. Reviving admiration is not complicated. You fell in love with this person and committed yourself to them; you come to these pages with a desire for that love to go on. You have positive feelings in there. Thinking about them and talking about them will bring them back to life more quickly and vividly than you might imagine. A plant that is wilting away often needs just a splash of water to leap back up toward the sun. A little bit goes a long way.

Today's exercise has three parts:

Step One: If you were to paint a verbal portrait of your partner in words, which words would you choose? Circle three to five choices:

Warm / Funny / Generous / Calm / Creative / Passionate / Intense / Vivacious / Thoughtful / Spontaneous /

Adventurous / Fun-loving / Playful / Astute / Perceptive / Nurturing / Sexy / Intelligent / Talented / Affectionate / Competent / Charming / Wise / Loving / Considerate / Attractive / Dependable / Flexible / Supportive / Curious / Interesting / Kind / Brave / Open / Easygoing / Sensitive

Step Two: Today, anytime you are together, notice the ways your partner embodies those qualities you circled above.

As you did yesterday, closely observe your partner when you're with them. Notice when they are demonstrating those qualities you love and appreciate. And then . . .

Step Three: Express it!

How often do you communicate to your partner the core, essential things you love and appreciate about them? Do it more, because every time counts!

Troubleshooting

Not much time to observe each other today?

Look at the words you circled above, and think of a time you can recall when your partner embodied one of those qualities. It could be from yesterday or a decade ago. It could be something huge (*You were supportive when you moved across the country with me for my dream job*) or something small (*You were really sexy in those jeans you wore yesterday!*). See if you can think of something specific for each of the three things. Then share with each other what memories came to mind. You may be surprised at the things your partner notices and appreciates about you, and vice versa.

Feeling shy or hesitant?

Write it down! Do the above activity (take the three words you circled, then think of three incidents that illustrate those qualities) and write it out as a journal activity. Write it like a letter, addressed to your partner. *You showed me how loyal you are when you . . . The first time I realized how adventurous you are was when you . . .*

When you're done, read your list to your partner—out loud! When we run this activity with couples in workshops, it's amazing the shift that happens in the room. It's irresistible. People break out into smiles and laughter. People who came in hesitant or self-conscious relax and warm up. The body language between couples changes noticeably. Even for people who came in unhappy or worried, you can see it again: that spark.

DAY 5

ASK FOR WHAT YOU NEED

JAKE WAS UPSET. IT HAD BEEN WEEKS SINCE HE AND HIS PARTNER, Miriam, had sat down to dinner together. And yet again, it was late in the evening and she was still at work. She'd texted, as she had so many nights, to say that she wouldn't be making it home for dinner. *Go ahead and eat without me, sweetie,* she'd typed. *I'll be at the studio late tonight!*

He understood. At least, he *had,* until recently. Miriam, an artist who did mixed-media sculptures, had gotten a big break: a gallery show at the university where she taught. She had been working hard to get ready for the show. But it was still months away. Meanwhile, Jake had a lot on his plate, too. After years of working in land use law for a firm that sucked up every spare minute of his time, he'd launched his own firm out of his living room. He loved being his own boss. There was still a lot to do, and now he had to handle everything himself, but his time was his own again. He could go for a bike ride on a beautiful day if he wanted, and make up the hours late at night. It was great. But lately it felt lonely—Miriam was never around, no matter when he took his time off. She'd always been supportive of him, all those years when he had to work crazy hours and pay his dues, and he wanted to be just as supportive now that she was in the make-or-break moment of her career. But several times in the past week alone, she'd brushed off his requests to spend time together, and he was starting to feel like he was the last thing on her to-do list. They were both driven, ambitious people, and they'd always been proud of how they lifted each other up professionally, how accommodating and understanding they were when the other had to make a big push. But before, it had always felt like the relationship came first. It didn't feel like that anymore. Maybe he wasn't as important to her as he thought. Maybe their marriage wasn't something she needed, now that she was ascending in the professional realm.

When Miriam did finally arrive home, late, Jake was wound tight as a wire.

"You know, you could have taken an hour off tonight, for once," he said. "I was really looking forward to dinner tonight. I went out and got your favorite—steamed clams."

"You did?" Miriam was surprised. "I had no idea. We've just been doing takeout and stuff lately, since we've both been so busy."

"I asked you yesterday if you wanted to come home for dinner, and you said yes!"

"Well of course I said that I *wanted* to! I thought maybe if I got enough done this afternoon after class, I'd be able to. I just can't right now, Jake. I have so much to do for the opening. I'm not ready at all. I thought you understood. I thought we were on the same page."

"OK. I know. I get that. I just thought that if I invited you to have dinner with me just *once* in an entire month, you'd make it happen. That is, if our relationship is still important to you."

"Of *course* our relationship is still important to me! Where on earth is this coming from?"

Pause. What's the problem here? Let's do an X-ray of this argument. Miriam thinks the two of them are "on the same page" about both being in an "all work and no play" phase. Jake thinks he invited Miriam to a date night dinner and she blew him off. If we rewind to the day before, this is what we'd see: Miriam packing a bag for the long day ahead as Jake talks about how things are going at the new law firm of "Jake and Miriam's Living Room" (he's still brainstorming names for his new firm)— it's going great, but he misses the way they used to meet up for dinner at different restaurants in the city after a long day at their respective offices. It was such a wonderful way to end the day— it really felt like he could leave everything back at the office when he'd walk into a crowded bar and see her sitting there with two glasses of wine, waiting for him.

"It would be nice to do that again," he says.

"Definitely," Miriam replies.

"Maybe we could do something tomorrow night," Jake says. "We could stay in, I'll cook!"

"Sure, maybe!" Miriam replies. "Text me later. I have to run." She kisses him and is out the door.

In this interaction, Jake and Miriam are having two completely separate conversations. It's almost like they're speaking two different languages—each thinking they understand the other, while the real meaning is lost. Jake believes he has expressed himself; he misses the dinners they used to have before their lives changed. That time specially reserved for just for the two of them was invaluable to him. He needs it, and feels disconnected from her without it. He knows that her work is important (his is, too!) and they're both busier than they've ever been, but he needs her to carve out an hour just for him, so that he doesn't feel like they're two boats drifting away from each other in a strong current. Hey, maybe making that time would even be helpful for both of them, even if it takes time away from work. Talking about their passion projects has always been a way for them to not only connect intimately with each other, but also support each other in those pursuits.

The problem is, Jake hasn't actually *asked* her.

Your partner isn't a mind reader. We all know this. And yet, what we see from so many couples is that we behave as if they were. We want our partners to pick up on little hints and signals about what we need and desire—or to just know. Jake dropped about a million hints, to clue Miriam in to how urgently he wanted to spend time with her. But his actual request was off-the-cuff casual. *Maybe we could do something tomorrow night.* Then he heard her "sure," but not her "maybe."

Miriam didn't realize what was being asked of her. She failed to fulfill Jake's desire. And when she didn't show up, he felt hurt, ignored, and resentful. The only explanation he could come up with was that he didn't matter to her as much as her work. And she felt surprised and annoyed when he was upset with her for not showing up. After all, she hadn't committed to anything. She'd only said "maybe." Perhaps if he'd expressed his need more clearly, she could have responded more clearly.

When you sit and stew on what your partner isn't doing, it can plant a seed of resentment that spreads like a weed. Resentment is hard to rip out once it's widespread—it's much harder to eradicate it than it is to prevent it from taking hold in the first place. But either way, the antidote is the same: you have to tell your partner what you need and want. But asking for what you need isn't always easy.

Why Does It Feel So Hard?

We've been taught that needs are bad. Needs are a weakness. We've been socially conditioned not to acknowledge our own needs, and even if we do, not to announce them. Women are taught, *Don't be too needy*. Men are taught, *You should be tough and strong and NOT have needs*. Both of these cultural messages are rooted in what we are taught is attractive and acceptable; what's feminine and what's masculine, and depending on our gender, what we should embody.

As fiercely as we may push back against these stereotypes, they continue to wield power over us even today. This is the cultural water we swim in; we absorb some of this messaging, no matter how hard we try to detox from it. Women have been trained to be nurturers—to satisfy the needs of others. But what happens to their needs? Men have been trained to be providers—to be strong, to not need help. But what happens to their needs?

Many of us have had our needs or requests ignored early in life, no matter what our gender is, which ingrains the belief that our needs aren't important or valid. So we are all moving through life with these subterranean needs and desires, suppressing instead of expressing them. And the trouble is, they find a way to rear their furry little heads, no matter how much we push them down. They'll shape our emotions and constrain our thinking. They'll influence our actions in ways that we might not be aware of. Suppressed needs can flare up into resentments and arguments when the unmet need simply becomes too much to keep inside—as we saw with Jake and Miriam.

We tiptoe around our needs instead of stating them outright because it feels safer. It can be nerve-racking to be so vulnerable—even with your partner. It can feel scary. If you ask someone for something, there's a chance they'll say no. At some point in our lives, we've all been shot down. And that can feel pretty bad. It can be hurtful and humiliating to say what you need or want and then be rejected. We'll do anything to avoid feeling that way—to the point where we'll avoid asking our partners directly for the simplest of things: *I'd love it if you could make time to have dinner with me* tonight. *I really need to spend some time with you—even just an hour. Can you make it work?* We prefer to hint and maneuver, hoping that the stars align, that our partners intuit our desires, and that we get what we most want without having to expose ourselves.

When we have had our needs ignored early in life, it teaches us one of two things:

1. We're not worthy of having our needs met, or
2. Needs are weak and bad.

We need to overturn this and flip the script. We are all worthy of asking for and receiving what we need. And needs are not a sign of weakness. Needs are normal, healthy, and human. They are as natural as breathing. They are like oxygen. Your physical and emotional needs are just as essential to your life and well-being as the food you eat, water you drink, and air you breathe. And so are your desires! We are often much too rigid about what we categorize as a need. You may ask yourself: *Is it a want or a need?* Our answer: It doesn't matter! We have a misconception that wants are not as valid as needs. Wants, we've internalized, mean you're greedy or selfish. *Not true.* Wants and needs exist across a nuanced range, and like colors across the light spectrum, there are almost infinite possibilities—from yellows to reds to blues to violets and from our most urgent needs to our deepest desires. They are all valid. And they should be expressed—especially to your partner.

It's OK to say what you want and need.

In fact, it's more than OK. It's *essential.*

Where We Go Wrong

Here's what happens in distressed relationships, over and over: We all have needs. We all have valid desires. But we don't say them. We drop hints. We suggest. We stay safely in the shadows. We hope our partners will "just know." We tell ourselves a story about why they should be able to figure it out without us having to say it ("It's obvious! It's just common sense!"), and we believe it. Then, when our partners fail to magically fulfill those needs, we feel resentful. We begin to believe that our partners don't care, are thinking only about themselves, are too busy for us, or no longer value the relationship as they once did. And so we criticize them.

You always.

You never.

These red flag phrases alert us that a couple is in shaky territory: the negative perspective might be starting to set in. They're scanning for what's wrong, and losing the capacity to notice what's right. And the end result is criticism, which is when we take aim at *who someone fundamentally is,* instead of distinguishing between the person and the action. Example: "I wish you wouldn't leave your socks on the living room floor" becomes "You are such a slob. You always leave your stuff all over the house. You never help me clean up." Even though these last two sentences don't include direct criticism, words like *always* and *never* are criticisms because they imply a personality flaw. After all, if "you always" do something wrong or "never" do something right, there must be something bad about you, right?

If we do manage to state our needs, we often feel we have to justify them by pointing out a deficit—something the other person isn't doing for us, or is lacking. We've been taught we shouldn't have needs, so the urge to justify is hard to overcome. "Because of your diet, I haven't been able to eat my favorite foods, so I'm going out to eat tonight!" This comes out as a criticism of the other person ("because of *your* diet") when this partner could have simply said, "I'd love to eat out tonight. I'm tired and could use a treat."

When we store up resentment and criticism instead of just asking for what we need, at some point, the dam has to break. It's like a reservoir of bad feelings, getting fuller and fuller, until all it takes is one little jostle and the whole thing comes crashing down. The tiniest thing can set it off; a minor disagreement suddenly becomes World War III. We call this "sandbagging": you pile up all your resentments, and then you ambush your partner with them. "Jim, we need to have a talk. You're a terrible father, you're awful in bed, and the worst thing about you is, you *don't recycle!*"

When we haven't asked clearly for what we need, criticism becomes a last line of defense. But it's not effective. Quite the opposite. People will use the phrase "constructive criticism"—it's a myth. There's no such thing as constructive criticism—criticism is always *destructive.*

All of this can be headed off with one simple fix: *Ask for what you need.*

Let Your Partner Shine for You

Remember: you don't need to justify a need. And never use criticism to frame your needs. It's a tactic we all tend to fall back on: we justify our own needs by first pointing out what's wrong with our partner's behavior. The logic is that if we've been wronged, then it's only fair to state our need or make a demand. The first healthy action you can take is to is *unlock yourself from this mindset*. You don't need to find a problem in order to justify your needs or wants.

If your partner feels attacked or criticized by you, you're not likely to get very far. It's not great for either of you to criticize, in fact; you sabotage yourself from being listened to and having your needs fulfilled before you've even begun. This doesn't mean you need to sweet-talk or manipulate your partner. But it does mean you need to be honest, clear, and proactive instead of *re*-active.

How do we do this effectively? Just follow this simple template:

First: Always describe yourself—not your partner. Don't ask for what you need by telling your partner what they're doing wrong. Don't even start by talking about your partner at all! This is about *you*, not them.

Second: Describe the situation you're upset about—not your partner's personality flaws. Talk about the events or circumstances that are bothering you or that you want to be different. This can allow your partner to *help* you in improving those conditions, instead of feeling defensive and attacked.

Third: State your positive *need*. What can your partner do for you to make you feel better? Be specific. Be clear. And keep it positive! Don't point out what your partner is doing wrong, or what they're *not* doing right. It's too easy to veer into criticism here. Instead, think of your request as an opportunity for your partner to do something right for you that you will really appreciate. *Tell your partner how to shine for you.*

Here are some examples of the wrong way versus the right way to say things:

> *Don't say:* "You never make time for me anymore. Obviously you couldn't care less about our relationship."

> *Do say:* "I feel lonely [your feeling] when we go this long without really spending quality time with each other [the

situation]. Can we find some time to just be together?"
[your positive need]

Don't say: "You always leave the kitchen such a mess.
What a slob you are! Don't you think I want to relax at the
end of the night, too?"

Do say: "I feel overwhelmed lately [your feeling] by all
there is to do around the house [the situation]. Could you
take over the dishes or laundry this week?" [your positive
need]

Flip the Script!

Let's take a look at a couple of scenarios, and how we can
flip the script.

Scenario 1: Your mother-in-law is coming over for dinner
tonight, and she always finds something to criticize you
about. (*The dinner is late. Your kids get too much screen
time. Did you have to buy a new car, in this economy?*) You
want your partner to stick up for you this time—last time,
it felt like you were just hung out to dry.

You say:

    a. "Your mother is a wart on the backside of humanity!
       You always take her side. I guess you must have the
       same bad opinion of me that she does."

Now flip it!

> a. "You know, I'm feeling anxious about your mother vis-iting tonight. She always seems to find something to criticize me about. Would you stick up for me tonight if she starts it? It would mean a lot."

Scenario 2: You've been cooking dinner every night for the past decade. It's getting old! You want your partner to do something different tonight. You don't have a big budget for eating out, so it's usually only a special occasion kind of thing. But it really feels like you're being taken for granted. And you just want a break.

You say:

> a. "I guess you're too cheap to take me out to dinner."

Flip it!

> a. "I'm tired of cooking. And it's been a long time since we had an excuse to go out. Let's go out tonight!"

It's simple. It's straightforward. And the beauty is, it works.

When we watch a couple start a conversation, we can accu-rately predict how that discussion will go. Will it be productive?

Will both people feel heard? Will the couple be kind to each other, even if they disagree? Will they reach a satisfying resolution? Or will there be acrimony, destructive criticism, defensiveness, and attacks? Ninety-six percent of the time, the outcome of not only the conversation but also the relationship six years down the line can be predicted by looking at these *first three minutes*.[1]

How you start a conversation matters. No matter how legitimate your need, if you begin with a harsh start-up (a criticism, or a "you always" or "you never" statement), you're putting yourself (and your partner!) at a huge disadvantage: not only will neither of you get what you want or need, but you may do damage to your relationship—especially if the harsh start-up becomes a habit. The alternative that we call "softened start-up" is an enormously helpful tool. How you start a conversation sets the tone for how you finish it. Begin without criticism. With compassion. Think about what your partner needs to hear in order to really listen to what you need and hopefully respond in a positive way. In a six-year longitudinal study, we found that the way couples began a problem-solving conversation was a huge predictor of whether or not they would stay happily partnered six years later.

So what happened with Miriam and Jake? Well, they're doing just fine. When they talked about it, Miriam discovered that Jake had been hesitant to ask her specifically to take time off work because he had a long history of being burned in that department. Growing up, his father often chose work over spending time with Jake or showing up at his events, even when he promised, even when Jake begged him to come. With every no-show, he'd felt crushed. And so he'd stopped putting himself out there. If he didn't ask, he wouldn't have to feel let down. He wouldn't have to feel like he was a low priority for someone he loved.

Of course, he *did* feel let down anyway—but he hadn't even given Miriam the chance to show up for him. In the end, it wasn't hard for her to rearrange things to make time for a couple of evenings a week when she put down her sculpting tools and came home for dinner, even during the busy run-up to her gallery opening. All she'd needed to know was how important it was.

"Are You Available?"

Timing matters. If you're going to talk to your partner about something important to you, you might feel brushed off or ignored if they aren't ready to engage the moment you are. And the stars may not simply align here: our data show that over the course of a typical day, busy couples have limited time together. In that window of time, the odds that you are both "turning toward" at the same time are low. Even if people are turning toward bids a majority of the time (60 percent), the chances that *both* partners are turning toward is only 36 percent. And even among the happily married couples we studied in the Love Lab, people whose bids for connection were not noticed or responded to would *rebid only 22 percent of the time.*[2] So, if you're wanting to point out a pretty garden you're passing as you drive together, maybe it's no big deal. If you have a rich history of turning toward, you're going to have a nice deep cushion in your emotional bank account, and missed bids will just roll off you like water off a duck. But if you're itching to engage deeply with your partner about something important, you probably need to be more intentional.

One couple figured out an effortless, ingenious way to handle the ubiquitous possibility of crossed wires and hurt feelings. Rachel and Jason had been together for twenty-seven years. They had two teenage daughters. And they remember well the early years of working two full-time jobs and parenting two little kids who needed their attention. Jason had always been a morning person; Rachel a night owl. When they did finally overlap and get some time together, it was gobbled up by logistics.

"We rarely had any time where we could talk about anything besides, 'Who's going to the grocery store? Who's picking up the kids?'" Rachel said. "Once you deal with schedules and food, who has the bandwidth for anything else?"

The problem was, when one person did need to talk, the other was often in work mode, or parent mode, or just exhausted. There were irritable spats and misunderstandings. Hurt feelings lingered.

Then one day, dropping off her daughter at Montessori school, Rachel overheard the teacher giving the kids a gentle instruction: If they wanted to talk to a friend when that friend was engaged in play or some other activity, they should first ask them, "Are you available?" The friend was then free to say yes or no, or "After I'm done with this drawing." The amazing thing was, the kids did it! Rachel laughed—it was so simple, basic, and elegant, a child could do it.

She and Jason tried it out. This was the new rule: if she wanted to talk to him about something important (or vice versa), she'd say, "Are you available?" It immediately brought a level of ease to interactions that had previously been more fraught. There was no guilt in saying "In ten minutes," or "After I finish this email."

"It made us pay attention to the moment," Rachel said. Jason added, "It takes the pressure off. And when you are ready to engage, you can give your full attention. Everything just goes better."

Try it today: *Are you available?*

TODAY'S PRACTICE

ASK FOR WHAT YOU NEED . . . BY DESCRIBING YOURSELF!

We all need to learn how to say what we want and need. It can feel uncomfortable or wobbly at first, but it's like riding a bike—once you get started, you'll quickly get the hang of it.

Today, your practice has three steps.

Step One: Reflect.

What do you need or want? Take a moment, right now, and think about what you've been wanting from your partner. Are you longing to spend more time with them? Do you need help with housework? Do you need to feel more supported in pursuing your career? Do you need to hear "I love you" more often?

Step Two: Reframe.

If you are thinking in the negative perspective, *flip it*. Don't point out what's wrong. Offer an opportunity. What is the *positive need* you would like them to fulfill?

Step Three: Describe yourself.

Always ask for what you need by talking about how you feel and what you need.

"I miss you. Can we hang out tonight, no phones and no TV?"

"I am absolutely swamped this week. Could you take something off my plate?"

"I'm feeling so tired today. Would you do bedtime with the kids tonight so I can rest for a few minutes? Then let's sit and have a glass of wine."

"I love being held by you. Give me a hug?"

Know what you need, say what you need, and you'll very likely get what you need! Your partner wants to be there for you—so let them. Make it easy! A common phrase comes to mind that people will often say with a whiff of sarcasm when someone doesn't guess exactly what they want: "Do I need to draw you a map?"

We say: *Yes!* Draw them a map. You'll both be happier for it.

Troubleshooting

When they feel attacked no matter how you ask . . .

Sometimes, no matter how great a job you do, your partner will interpret a statement of your want or need as a criticism—even if you do your best to phrase it as a positive need. That happens when there's been a pattern of criticism in the past, and when resentment has really built up over time. It happens when there's been a lot of turning away from each other's needs, too. Now there's emotional distance and a default habit of scanning for what's wrong, what's missing, or what's not perfect. If you're that deep into the negative perspective, your partner can look at you longingly and say "I love you," and all you will hear is criticism.

But you *can* change it.

When you stop phrasing your needs and desires in critical terms, and instead replace them with softened start-ups and positive requests, you can quickly melt the ice. Your partner may be wary at first, and continue to hear criticism at every turn; you may then hear defensiveness in their response. If you do, the next time you make a request, be explicit. "I really do not want to criticize you here. I just want to say, I would love it if . . . [and state your *positive* need]."

Start slow.

Some couples need to ease into this. If today's practice feels too difficult, try this instead: Rather than asking for a corrective (something they aren't doing that you want them to do; something you want them to do better or differently), just ask for something that would make you happy. Ask them to sit and watch a movie with you. Ask them to stop at the bakery on the way home and bring you your favorite treat. Ask them to fix that special drink they make so well. Ask them for a hug! Make a sweet request that they can easily fulfill, so you can genuinely say "Thank you! That felt great!"

DAY 6

REACH OUT AND TOUCH

GRACE AND ANDREW WERE WORRIED ABOUT THEIR SEX LIFE. IT WAS AT an all-time low. They couldn't exactly pinpoint why—they weren't fighting. They got along fine. Yes, they were busy, but who wasn't? Andrew worked at the nearby military base, in technology. A computer whiz, he loved when people asked what he did for work, so that he could give the answer that always made their ears perk up: "It's classified." Grace stayed home to raise their three young kids . . . as well as a flock of chickens, ducks, and soon (she hoped) goats. Their house was a colorful swirl of chaos—Grace, an artist and musician (she used to teach elementary school), led her kids through painting projects, guitar lessons, and cooking classes. Andrew came home, tossed his tie over his shoulder and cooked dinner while she cleaned out the chicken coop, or moved the interminable laundry to the dryer, all as the kids played and chased and fought and yelled. It was busy, it was loud, it was exhausting—but they were happy! Weren't they? They both were starting to wonder. The sexual energy that had once drawn them toward each other like magnets seemed to have evaporated into thin air. They were becoming more like amiable partners running a business than like lovers.

They'd gone through droughts before when each of their children was born, but they'd always bounced back after. Now, their youngest was almost three years old. Everybody was sleeping at night now. There were no more babies waking up; no more toddlers crawling in between them. And yet, the fun, sweet, spontaneous sexual connection they'd previously enjoyed remained elusive. The season of sex should have returned, it seemed, and yet like some strange weather pattern, it hadn't.

They'd tried a handful of strategies, like going out on a date, or scheduling a night to rendezvous in the bedroom, but it felt forced, and half the time, when they got in bed together, they just ended up going to sleep.

Andrew: "I'll be thinking all day, *We are definitely having sex tonight!* But half the time she falls asleep before I even finish brushing my teeth. Or I fall asleep while she's checking on the kids. Or we start talking about bills or what we have to do tomorrow and it kills the mood."

"But there's not even any mood to kill!" Grace says. "We get in bed together, and all of a sudden it feels weird to just start making out. I mean, we haven't even had the chance to hold hands all day or even just have a conversation. So I bring up something to talk about and somehow we never get around to the fun and the sex part."

She added: "It just doesn't seem fun anymore. It used to. And I want it to be like it used to! I don't want to have to try so hard."

Another couple, Alicia and Abdul, have a very different life from Andrew and Grace's, yet share the same problem. Their sleek apartment is nestled right in the heart of downtown Seattle. They work as lawyers for two of the area's tech companies. Their passions are biking and travel. Now in their early forties, they haven't had kids and don't plan to.

When the city went into lockdown during the coronavirus pandemic, Alicia and Abdul looked for an upside: they'd have a lot more time for each other.

But as the pandemic year unfolded, things started to change. Home all day, on conference and Zoom calls, they felt dull and disconnected at the end of the day. The coffee shops and restaurants they used to go to had shuttered. They were both tired of cooking—they kept making the same things. They spent a great deal of time watching TV. They'd blown through all the prestige television series across all their various streaming services. They were trapped together in the same small apartment—and yet they were spending *less* time together. How was it possible? Neither one of them felt much like having sex. They felt like roommates. What was Alicia thinking about? Did Abdul even *want* to cuddle, or did he want his space?

Is This "Normal"?

It's natural to worry, and to wonder: *Are other people going through this? Or is it just us?* Chrisanna Northrup, coauthor of *The Normal Bar: The Surprising Secrets of Happy Couples and What They Reveal about Creating a New Normal in Your Relationship,* was experiencing just this type of scenario when she launched into the project that would become her book. She was a busy mom and entrepreneur, starting a wellness business, when her relationship with her husband of fifteen years hit "the blahs." As she struggled to figure out how to address the problem, she found herself wondering if other couples were dealing with the same thing—where did she and her husband fall on the spectrum of "normal" in relationships? And, if they were allegedly normal, what were *they* doing to fix the problem? What *was* normal when it came to communication, sex, conflict, and more?

She enlisted the help of two of the most prominent sociologists in the US, Dr. Pepper Schwartz and Dr. James Witte, to get to the bottom of "normal" in modern love. These scientists had gathered a *lot* of data, from all around the world, to determine what was "universal" about relationships—across nationality, sexuality, race, socioeconomics, and more. Volunteers from twenty-three countries responded to a survey with over thirteen hundred questions designed to answer our burning questions about long-term relationships, including a particularly hot topic: Who out there has a great sex life, and how do they keep that flame going through the years?

You might guess that the couples with the hottest sex lives were the ones who said yes to sex when their partner initiated it, or the ones who incorporated unusual new ways to spice things up, or the ones who were up for anything in the bedroom. Nope. In fact, what happened *in* the bedroom, once couples slid between the sheets, had very little to do with how satisfied partners were with their sex lives. Northrup, Schwartz, and Witte identified specific habits practiced by those in happy, thriving relationships where both partners were satisfied sexually.[1]

1. They say "I love you" every day, and mean it.
2. They kiss passionately for no reason at all.
3. They give each other compliments (and surprise romantic gifts!).
4. They know what turns their partner on and off erotically.
5. They are physically affectionate, even in public.
6. They keep playing and having fun together.
7. They cuddle—*often*.
8. They make sex a priority, not the last item of a long to-do list.
9. They stay good friends.
10. They can talk comfortably about their sex life.
11. They have weekly romantic dates.
12. They take romantic vacations.
13. They are mindful about turning toward.

Don't be overwhelmed by this list! If you feel like you could use improvement in some of the areas listed above, remember: *you're already working on this.* All of the practices we've been asking you to incorporate into your routine this week are here: Offering compliments. Being curious and asking questions that really go places. Putting time for each other at the top of your to-do list instead of at the bottom. And notice: the vast majority of habits on this list happen long before you and your partner end up in bed together, even the ones that involve physical affection. Today, this is what we're going to focus on: *touch*.

Touch is a powerful drug. Physical intimacy has a physiological effect on the body—it releases oxytocin, the hormone that helps with bonding and connection. It's what bonds mothers and babies together just after birth. When oxytocin hits the bloodstream, we experience all kinds of beneficial effects. It lowers blood pressure, washes away stress, even reduces your risk of heart disease.[2] Touch is not just good for your relationship; it's good for your physical health and longevity. For us humans, it's as necessary as water, as food—even as the air we breathe.

Touch Is Like Oxygen . . .

We can't survive without it. Physical touch is critical to our survival as a species. Humans, as we've said, are pack animals—we die without one another, without connection, without physical contact. We discovered long ago that if you take a human infant and isolate her, she has a greater chance of dying, even if you give her all the food and water she needs.[3]

Those of us in the field of psychology were reminded of this recently, during the COVID-19 pandemic. People were self-isolating and quarantining, in alignment with instructions from the Centers for Disease Control. But a lot of people don't live with family and aren't coupled up. They were alone. As the weeks stretched into months, then to a full year, the effects of isolation took their toll. Many people who'd been quarantining alone began to experience "touch deprivation,"[4] which researcher Dr. Tiffany Field says is strongly linked to anxiety and depression.[5] Other studies have referred to this effect as "touch starvation," an apt phrase to describe what happens when we don't have a regular diet of physical contact. While welcome physical touch releases oxytocin, which shifts the body into "rest and repair" mode, touch starvation does the opposite. Stress goes up. Anxiety goes up. This causes the overproduction of cortisol—a helpful metabolic hormone in the correct dosage, but when there's too much in the bloodstream, it shoots you into fight-or-flight mode. Heart rate increases, blood pressure rises, breathing becomes shallow. Over time, it can interfere with digestion and even suppress the immune system. Touch starvation can, quite literally, make you sick.[6]

Field, a developmental psychologist, currently heads the Touch Research Institute at the University of Miami. She has called touch "the mother of all senses." Field herself had a firsthand experience with the potency of human touch. In the mid-1970s, when she was a graduate student, she gave birth to her daughter a month early, at thirty weeks. At the time, the accepted medical knowledge was that premature babies should not be touched—the risk of infection was too high. They were keeping babies in incubators; there was no contact between parents and infants. But Field believed that touch could help her daughter thrive. She convinced the hospital staff to let her massage her daughter, and found that the baby became calmer and ate more. She began working to develop an incubator that hospitals could use for premature babies that would allow parents to touch and connect with their babies physically, while also keeping the baby antiseptically incubated and shielded from infection. She ran a study and found that when parents touched their premature infants, the babies thrived, gained weight faster, and were discharged from the hospital almost a full week earlier.[7]

It's not just infants who benefit so profoundly from physical touch and connection. We ran a study on adults among couples who were expecting their first child. We found that fifteen minutes of touch per day—in the form of a neck or shoulder massage for the woman who was pregnant—had a profound impact on the rates of postpartum depression (PPD) after birth. In couples who practiced the fifteen minutes of massage per day, 22 percent of the new mothers showed signs of PPD. In the group that did not practice touch? The incidence of PPD shot up to 66 percent. Just fifteen minutes of massage, of physical touch and physical connection, made that difference.[8]

We thrive on touch—and it doesn't have to be sexual. Sex is an important part of a relationship, but complicated for some. Many people think that the only way to experience touch is through sex or activities that lead to sex—not true. Research shows that people of all genders who cuddle have more satisfying long-term relationships.

OK—so touch is good for us. It's good for our health. It's good for our relationships. Data show that casual touch between couples—holding hands, kissing, being physically affectionate in public or really anytime—correlates with a thriving sex life. We know how great it is . . . so what gets in the way?

Touch Taboos and Other Obstacles

We bring all kinds of stuff with us into a relationship. An influential factor is the culture we grew up with. For a lot of us, this is something we've never paused to think about—but some cultures are more touch-averse than others.

In the 1960s, the researcher Sidney Jourard conducted a now-famous field study that has come to be called "the coffee-house study." He traveled around the world, parked himself in coffee shops, and observed the couples who came in. He counted how many times, in one hour, the couples touched each other in any way: holding hands; stroking each other's arm, back, or hair; knees leaning together; and so on. What he found: In Paris, France, couples touched each other an average of 110 times an hour. In Gainesville, Florida, they touched twice an hour. And in London, England, zero times. Jourard concluded that certain cultures (including ones many of us have lived within our whole lives) seem to have a "touch taboo."[9]

If culture is the larger ocean we swim in, then family is the smaller pond. How you were raised versus how your partner was raised can impact your comfort level with touch and your physical touch–related needs. If either of you grew up in a low-touch or even no-touch household, then physical touch—even from a life partner—can be uncomfortable or anxiety provoking. In some cases, when people have experienced abuse, touch can trigger fear, even if it's kind, loving touch. This can make touch "double-edged": it can be wonderful, comforting, arousing, but it can feel threatening if it's done quickly, too roughly, or by surprise. We have to be conscious of our partners' backgrounds, and the way they've been touched (or not!) in the past.

Our romantic relationships don't exist in a vacuum—our habits surrounding touch are influenced by an array of factors that may at first be invisible to us. There are all kinds of reasons why we each have different "settings" when it comes to what kind of touch, and how much touch, we're comfortable with and need. But no matter where you are on the spectrum, you can incorporate more loving touch into your life with your partner in a way that feels good to you. You don't have to be alone and self-quarantining in a global pandemic to experience what some psychologists refer to as "skin hunger": an acute need for more touch than you are currently getting.

Are there differences in the need for touch and desire for sex between men and women? The stereotype is certainly that men tend to want sex more than women do. Is it true? Well, sort of. On average, research shows that in a typical day, men think about sex twice as often as women do.[10] But everyone is different. Plenty of heterosexual relationships flip the script on this one, where the woman has a higher sex drive than the man does. Women in particular may wonder about their libido as they age—it's natural to worry if you feel your sex drive is waning. We counsel many women who are wondering, *What's wrong with me?* We can tell you confidently: *nothing.* The reality is that it's not unusual for women to begin to lose their sex drive. Let's not forget that in prehistoric times, the human life expectancy was about age forty.[11] Women didn't need a sex drive later in life because they didn't *have* a "later." But here's the thing: positive, intimate, relaxing, nonsexual touch is great for us all in so many ways—including stirring up the heat of a libido that may be in a new and less active phase. What we've seen in the couples we've worked with: when men, or partners of women, approach the woman not *just* with pure sexuality but with positive nonsexual touch (cuddling, a massage, a foot rub), it's so relaxing and stimulating that it can lead to sexuality.

What this *doesn't* mean is that you should manipulate your partner into sex, or expect that every moment of physical connection or expression will lead to sex. What it also doesn't mean is that if someone doesn't want to have sex at the drop of a hat, they aren't interested in sex or wouldn't want to, ever. For many men (though not all), sexual desire leads to contact. For many women (again, not all), contact leads to sexual desire. Wherever you land on the sexual spectrum, you may recognize your own patterns in one of these descriptions. Many people can become aroused much more easily if the touch is nonsexual to begin with.

The point is *touch for the sake of touch.* Physical intimacy does not need to lead to sex for it to be worthwhile. One of the best things you can do is to erase the expectation that it will, or should. Touch is its own whole nutrient that both of your bodies need.

Talk about It!

The issues we discussed above—including culture, background, family, trauma—highlight the fact that it's important to not just practice touch, but to *talk* about it. We can be, even after years together, unaware of certain needs or preferences our partners have surrounding how or when they are touched. You may find it calming, for example, to be hugged and held when you're anxious or angry, but your partner may become agitated or frustrated by the very same gesture. In a moment like that, you can simply say, "What do you need right now? Would you like to be held, or do you want some space?" It comes down to communication: addressing where, when, and how you want to be touched.

Ask each other:

What kinds of touch do you most like?

What do you not like?

When is your favorite time to be touched or hugged?

Are there times when you don't want to be touched?

Are there some places you like to be touched more than others?

With the last question, we're talking more about nonsexual times. People will often have specific areas of their bodies that they most like to have massaged or rubbed, which they find relaxing or soothing, but their partners might not know about those.

When we see couples like Grace and Andrew, who want to bring more energy, passion, and spontaneity into their sex life, the number one thing we tell them to do is: *talk about it!* Have a conversation. You have to be able to talk about touch. If you're not used to addressing it head on, it can feel a little wobbly, like riding a bike. But try out the simple questions above and you'll soon get the hang of it.

And the second thing is: don't fixate on the bedroom! You'll notice that there's nothing in this week's practices that asks you to do anything specific when it comes to your sex life. That's because when it comes to sex, each relationship is wildly different. There is no magical number, no set data point, on how much sex you should be having in order to have a great, fulfilling, and long-lasting union. Models for success in that arena are all over the map. What we do know is that practicing these tiny habits—including affectionate touch—is going to ramp up your friendship, affection, appreciation, understanding, and trust. And yeah—you'll probably have more sex, too.

"The Trust Molecule"

Touch is powerful, even nonsexual touch. It's soothing. It helps you connect emotionally. It's not an illusion that when your partner takes your hand, you feel more attuned to them. The psychologist James Coan ran this experiment: A woman was put into an fMRI tube for a brain scan with an electrode attached to one of her big toes. Inside the tube, right where she could see it, a projector showed her one of two possible images: a green circle or a red x. When the red x appeared, a quarter of the time, she'd receive a mild electric shock. (It wasn't painful, but it wasn't pleasant.) What Coan saw on the brain scan was that when she was shown the red x, the anticipation of the electric shock would reliably turn on the fear system in her brain: her two amygdalae, down in the temporal lobe of the brain a few inches behind the eyes, would light up.

So then Coan introduced a twist. He set up a new condition and compared three scenarios: In the first, the woman's husband sat next to the fMRI tube and held her hand. In the second, a stranger held her hand. In the third, nobody held her hand—she was alone.

The results? With either no one or a stranger holding her hand, the fear system of the brain lit up just as before. But when her husband held her hand, the fear system shut down completely. She saw the red *x*, which should have triggered the anticipatory fear response—but it didn't.[12]

Coan ran the study again with same-sex couples and found the identical result. This was before the Supreme Court decision to legalize same-sex marriage, so Coan asked them: Did they consider themselves married? Were they committed to each other? If the answer was yes, they showed reduced fear response. Feeling committed was like protective armor against fear.[13]

Just holding hands—that's all it took. It's just a small, minimal touch, something we do casually, barely thinking about it—we reach out and take our partner's hand. And we could do it even more often. Even this simple touch is powerful, because like any welcome touch from someone you love, it causes oxytocin to be secreted into the bloodstream. Researcher Paul Zak calls oxytocin "the molecule of trust." How powerful is it? *Very*. Zak ran an experiment in which he gave people money and had them play a trust game that involved giving away money to other players: If you gave your money away, the amount itself tripled. But you had to trust the other person to funnel some of it back to you. On average, people would give away half the money they were given and keep the other half. They were fairly conservative. But then, squirt a little bit of oxytocin up their nose, and they gave away more. They immediately became more trusting.[14]

If you've ever made a bad decision in a relationship, or been swept off your feet by someone irresistible and utterly wrong for you, oxytocin may be to blame. It's also sometimes called "the hormone of bad judgment"—in another study, people under its intoxicating influence made poor investment decisions, trusting someone who was quite obviously a con man.[15] The point is, it's powerful! So use it for good—with your partner. And the power to do so is indeed in your hands, simply through touching each other. There's something else, Zak now says, that works just as well as a synthetic oxytocin nasal spray to get the love and bonding hormones flowing through your veins: a twenty-second hug.[16] Holding hands, a hug, a kiss, a few minutes of shoulder massage—they might seem like small actions, but they pack a lot of power. Here's what we tell people: Every chance you get, hug your partner for twenty seconds. And whenever you can snatch a moment, kiss for six seconds.

Why hug for twenty seconds? Because that's exactly how long it takes for oxytocin to metabolize in your bloodstream.

And why six, for the kiss? Well, that's just our intuition. And besides, it feels good!

The Magic of Mini-Touches

So what happened with Grace and Andrew? Those two had a solid foundation. But they were losing ground. They wanted more time for sex, for contact, for intimacy, but they didn't have the time, and they weren't making time. Their lives had split into two parallel lives—Andrew was at the base, doing his classified work; Grace was home setting up fingerpaints and teaching little fingers how to play chords on the guitar. In the evening, it was a sprint: to get dinner made, to get everybody bathed and in bed, and then to loop back to the computer for the inevitable final round of emails or paperwork. The bills, the dishes, the pets, the laundry. Sometimes, in the evening, they'd settle down to watch a favorite show on Netflix, one about a couple who has the most extreme long-distance relationship you could ever imagine: she's an astronaut on a three-year mission to Mars; he stays home at mission control and raises their daughter. Even when watching this show, they'd end up on separate pieces of furniture instead of together—Grace under a blanket on the couch, Andrew in an armchair across the room.

That their sex life seemed lackluster was a problem, sure, but it was the canary in the coal mine. They *missed* each other.

We worked on emotional connection. But they really needed the connection of physical touch to span the distance being created by their busy, separate lives. So what we started working on was *mini-touches*. Little quick touches as they were running by each other. A quick kiss. A squeeze on the shoulder. A hug.

We worked on how they welcome each other at the end of the day. This was the plan we came up with: whoever arrives home second (often it was Andrew, arriving from work, but sometimes it would be Grace and the kids coming home from errands or school pickup) throws open the door and announces, "I'M HERE!" And the first comes to the door and greets them with a hug and a kiss.

They loved it. It was fun. It was funny! The kids got into it.

They loved to run in the door and scream, "I'M HERE! I'M HERE!" They loved their parents standing in the middle of the chaos, giving each other a long hug.

They began to find all kinds of times to add in rituals for physical connection. In the morning, they started saying goodbye with a kiss—even if Andrew left early, he'd kiss her while she was sleeping. A German study, discussed in the book *The Science of Kissing*, found that men who kiss their wives goodbye in the morning live five years longer than men who don't.[17] Good night rituals are also wonderful whether you have sex that night or not. How *else* do you say good night to your partner? Kiss, hug, hold each other for a while and talk until everybody's drowsy and ready for sleep? This can be a sweet moment.

A recent study looked at 184 couples and investigated the link between emotional attachment and physical "touch satisfaction."[18] The focus was on *nonsexual* intimate touch: hugging, hand-holding, cuddling, and such. Unsurprisingly, they did indeed find a strong link. But what was really interesting is that people were all over the map in terms of touch needs and touch anxiety (wanting more than they were getting). But even when people reported that they *weren't* getting as much touch as they would like, their relationships were improved when they saw their partner making an effort. In other words, just seeing and feeling your partner making a point to reach out and connect physically was enough to give love a boost.

In the Love Lab, with those three thousand couples we observed, the patterns of physical connection were clear.[19] The successful couples—the ones who were still happily together six years later—were the ones who touched each other affectionately while they were cooking, cleaning, talking about the weather. They were the ones who held hands; the ones who touched each other encouragingly, even as they worked through a conflict; the ones who leaned toward each other rather than away, so that if you were to draw a line straight down from the crown of each of their heads, those lines would always be in the process of coming together, like the two descending sides of a drawbridge, about to connect.

TODAY'S PRACTICE

THE MAGIC OF MINI-TOUCH

To get that healing dose of oxytocin, you need to put the time in. But even little bits of time add up. A moment here, a moment there—they make a difference. They aggregate and build exponentially, strengthening your emotional and physical connection. So today's assignment is to *create as many moments of physical connection as possible*. This doesn't have to be about sex—just sitting together on the couch, holding hands, or stopping for a hug will all establish and nourish your physical connection and emotional closeness. What you do is up to you, and any amount is good. The more the better! But do talk about it with your partner and make sure you're both on board. This should be natural, comfortable, and fun. As long as everyone's all-in, then go for the whole list!

Kissing activates five out of twelve cranial nerves, and that's very good! And a twenty-second hug releases oxytocin into your bloodstream. Your blood vessels dilate. Your brain receives more oxygen. The physical effects are real. So go get that love hormone: it's good for your brain, your body, and your relationship.

How many of these can you pack into the day?

Check as many as you'd like!

❑ Kiss . . . for six seconds
❑ Hug. . . . for twenty seconds

❑ Hold hands . . . for as long as you like

❑ Trade a ten-minute massage (one person sits on the couch, the other on the floor in front of them . . . then swap)

❑ Cuddle on the couch

❑ Put an arm around your partner

❑ Touch each other's hand or arm while you're talking

❑ Put a hand on your partner's shoulder if they're stressed

❑ Touch foreheads

❑ Touch feet under the table

Reflect . . .

Now, toward the end of the day, spend a few minutes sharing with your partner how it felt to touch a little more that day—both giving and receiving touch. Was there any particular moment or type of touch that you really appreciated? What kind of touch felt best for you? What types of touch would you like to integrate more regularly into your relationship? Talk about how you could do so more consistently. You'll be glad you did.

Troubleshooting

If you feel pressured by touch . . .

We tend to think that if our partners are touching us a lot, they want sex, but that might not necessarily be true. One partner might just be looking for closeness and connection; the other perceives a desire for something more, doesn't want that in that particular moment, and pushes affectionate touch away.

To clear things up: Talk specifically about where affectionate touch stops and erotic touch begins. Where's that boundary for you? When your partner knows better what signals he or she is giving you in the way they're touching you, it can be easier to just enjoy affectionate touch without pressure, and to engage in erotic touch when welcome.

If you and your partner have different levels of touch needs . . .

Some people are less comfortable with touch or need less of it. Others crave it as a road to intimacy and to feeling accepted. Sometimes, we've worked with couples where a huge gulf in touch comfort becomes a serious problem. But usually, partners can learn to navigate each other's touch comfort. This can be cultural, as we discussed, and deeply ingrained.

If you get feedback from your partner that they would like less touch than what you've been initiating, don't take it as a rejection. Understand that people have different backgrounds and different childhood experiences. These experiences create an imprint of what you're comfortable with, and not comfortable with: whether your family was big on hugs and physical intimacy, for example, is incredibly formative. What we were raised with forms these deep footprints in our brains that we tend to step right into in our adult relationships.

So remember: one of our lifelong missions is to have compassion for these enduring vulnerabilities. It isn't your partner's fault that they feel this way. It's not a rejection of you. It's just the way it is. Here's a parallel: you have really light blue eyes and have to wear sunglasses, but your partner doesn't like that because they want to be able to look into your eyes. Well . . . there's nothing you can do about that. Accepting that it's nobody's fault, that this is just the way it is, can go a long way.

When touch is really touchy . . .

If you have a partner who has experienced unwanted touch in their past—whether sexual assault or abuse—you need to talk to them about what kinds of touch are OK and which are not. Talking about touch (instead of just guessing) is important for all couples, as we covered today, but especially crucial in this case. People who've experienced sexual trauma or abuse can certainly benefit from therapy, but issues surrounding which types of touch make them feel safe, relaxed, and turned on, versus the types that elicit a defensive, uncomfortable, or fearful response, may never be "fixed." So talk to your partner. "What's your favorite way that I touch you? Are there any ways I touch or hug you that you don't like?"

Julie, who has experienced sexual assault, doesn't like to be hugged from behind, or even surprised by touch. In our long marriage together, we've figured out ways around this. When John is coming in for a hug or snuggle and isn't sure whether Julie has spotted him, he says "Incoming!" When Julie hears that, his embrace is always welcome.

DAY 7

DECLARE A DATE NIGHT

LET'S TALK ABOUT LONELINESS IN MARRIAGE.

It sounds negative, but it's a fact of life for so many couples. So if you feel it, or have ever felt it, you aren't an outlier. This is common. We can spend years or decades together, raise kids, and occupy the same space, but instead of *sharing* a life as we intended, we're living parallel lives. We can find ourselves sitting in the same room with the person we married or committed to, the person we love, and feel very alone.

In 2002, the Sloan Center at UCLA launched a study like none that had ever been done before. They sent social scientists into the homes of busy families—dual-career couples with kids—who recorded each family's every waking moment over the course of one week. It was like a reality TV show before the era of reality TV: researchers with handheld cameras would follow people around from room to room, taping every interaction, conversation, and sigh. This was quite different from our Love Lab, where unobtrusive cameras captured the data, and couples could immediately feel alone with each other. Here, there was a living, breathing person standing in the same room with them, zooming in as participants hashed something out with their partner. It seems like the participants would feel awkward and self-conscious being observed, right?

Study participants later reported that, in fact, they *did* start to forget that someone else was there. As strange and invasive as it felt at first, the camera-carrying anthropologists quickly melted into the background, and participants were able to just be normal and natural in their homes. As a result, by the end of the weeklong study, the 1,540 hours of videotape that researchers amassed offered an accurate portrait of how couples operated in the real world: how much time they spent with each other, or with their children, or on household chores; their fights and their negotiations; their sweet moments and their bad ones, too. The cameras turned on as they woke and began preparing for the day, and didn't turn off until the last light was switched off.

The study was conducted in West Los Angeles, in middle-class neighborhoods.[1] Thirty-two families participated, and the sample captured LA's diversity: Black, Latino, Asian, and mixed-race families were profiled, along with several same-sex couples. The study became a treasure trove of data offering insight into how modern couples actually live. One thing that stuck out: husbands and wives were alone together in the same room only 10 percent of the time. But much more shocking was this fact: the average amount of time that couples spent in conversation with each other was a mere *thirty-five minutes per week*. And most of those conversations were about logistics: errands, bills, or who's going to do what. Hardly any of those conversations were about deeper subjects—the topics that are less urgent, but actually more important. There was no "How was your day?" Or, "How is your job going?" "Do you feel like you're doing too much?" "What's on your mind?" If they had dinner together, they were talking to the kids instead of to each other. (Valuable in its own right, but not the same as connecting as a couple.) It was clear by the end of the study that for the vast majority of couples, their lives had become this infinite to-do list, and they were neglecting the relationship that was at the center of it all.

The Sloan study focused on dual-income couples with kids, but we've seen this happen with every configuration: couples with kids where one stays home and the other goes to work; couples where both work; even couples where neither works because they've managed an early retirement or are taking time off. Couples without kids experience the same—we get work-oriented and exhausted; by the time we come home at night, we just want to crash on the couch and watch something on TV. We might be in the same room, but we aren't talking to each other.

There's nothing wrong with this. We all need to decompress and relax sometimes; other times, we need to get stuff done: get the kids into bed, run the laundry, catch up on work. That's life! But if we do this day after day, we lose track of who the other person is. Love maps begin to fade.

People change and evolve over time, and time goes by quickly—much more quickly than it might seem. Young couples with kids (but it's really true for all of us) will often put their heads down and just go, go, go. But if we don't look up and pause every so often to check where our partners are—what they're thinking about, what they're worried about, excited about, what they dream about—when we finally do stop and try to connect with them, they're going to feel really far away. It gets harder and harder to reach them, or for them to reach us.

We can be quite successful—paying the bills, working hard, getting everything done, excelling and working toward goals—but may spend so much time *not* focused on each other that we become really out of touch with each other, in every way. The Sloan study hit on something that is truly universal for couples everywhere: Once committed and settled down, they stop paying attention to the relationship. Other concerns seem more urgent and emergent. The relationship—that solid, foundational bedrock on which we build our adult lives—gets taken for granted. And without upkeep and maintenance, it can start to crack and crumble.

Go Out and Have Some Fun

We wanted to be able to better answer the questions: *Who goes for couples therapy? What drives them there?* We surveyed more than forty thousand couples, across different sexual orientations, who were about to begin therapy.[2] Eighty percent of them reported that "fun had come to die" in their relationship. They'd lost the ability to just enjoy each other.

Michele Weiner-Davis, a social worker and author, has written about "the sex-starved marriage," in which a couple's sex life has faded away.[3] In her experience, when couples come in for counseling, they don't often bring up their sex life as their number one complaint—there are other problems they present as the primary issue, such as the division of household labor, finances, or differences in parenting styles. But then it becomes apparent that they've lost touch with each other—physically, emotionally, and intellectually. They are living parallel lives that have stopped intersecting.

But what we've seen is that even when people go to sex therapy, often the sex therapy fails. Why? We theorize that the sex therapy sometimes feels too narrow. It's only a surface problem. It's not the core problem. The problem is bigger than sex. Yes, sexuality is missing. But so is sensuality, adventure, and *fun*. It's almost as if we've gotten the message that "adulting" means shutting down the imagination you had as a kid—the play, the imagination, the creativity. We come to believe that we need to let go of these "childish" pursuits in order to be successful. But a successful relationship is *built* upon these things. They're part of our best nature as humans. Our best art and thinking come from them; and our most intimate moments come from them, too. And yet moment to moment, day by day, they fall to the bottom of our long, long list of triaged priorities.

Many couples, without intending to, have shut down their openness to sensuality, adventure, and fun, and all the strategies we try with them go nowhere. They aren't responsive to touch, to open-ended questions, or to romantic overtures from their partners. They've even stopped enjoying great meals, or exploring new things to cook in the kitchen. The "sex-starved marriage" really isn't only about sex, fundamentally. It's one where people have, over time, shut down all forms of openness: to sensuality, to adventure, to play and silliness, to learning together. They've lost track of all of these reasons they got into the relationship to begin with: being close to each other physically, cuddling, having great conversations and relaxing together, dancing together, exploring together, and traveling together. It's all been slowly and gradually replaced by an infinite to-do list and eventually . . . loneliness takes the place of connection.

It happened to us at a certain point in our marriage. We were both insanely busy. John was teaching full-time, writing grants, and publishing papers. Julie spent a full forty hours a week in sessions with patients, and that didn't include the rest of the job: the paperwork, the preparation, and the research. We were both working at least sixty hours a week. We'd always been a busy, ambitious, two-career couple from the first moment we met—but now, it was all taking its toll. We were snappy with each other—irritable and short-tempered. At home, we moved apart instead of toward each other, like magnets flipped the wrong way. We had definitely stopped going on dates. We both had so much work to catch up on at night. And we were so tired. The *last* thing we wanted to do was go out.

But one day, we had yet another little fight about something—who knows what. The fight was really about something else. It was about how distant we were. How we weren't even touching each other anymore. Our relationship was starving for a lack of positive touch. And we suddenly realized that we didn't want to live like this.

We both agreed on one thing: We needed some time together. We needed a date. We were marriage experts—how many people had we advised on this very thing?

We got our calendars out and started flipping, looking for a day we both had free, but there was nothing but conflicts.

"Let's just go out tonight," John said. "Let's drop everything and go."

We cleared the evening. We got dressed up, like we had a party to attend, and went down to the Hotel Sorrento in downtown Seattle, a gorgeous old redbrick hotel that's been there since 1909 and has the lush, faded luxury of that era. We weren't guests there. But we pretended we were. We strode confidently in and commandeered a velvet couch right by the fireplace. We each ordered one drink, and then sat and talked for hours on that couch, while the fire flickered away by our feet. Other guests milled about, sat for a while, and left—we outlasted them all. Nobody noticed that we didn't belong or kicked us out. It was cheap and felt slightly illicit, which was a thrill. It was a great date.

The effect of that one date was, quite literally, immediate. Walking out of the hotel we felt transformed—sitting by that fire had reignited our own.

The next day, making coffee and packing up our lunches in the kitchen, we had the same conversations we always did about the logistics of the day—who was going where, when, how, and so on—but this time we felt like magnets flipped the right way again.

That one emergency date was so successful, we decided to make date night a weekly thing. No matter what, we would go. And we did. We'd be tired. We'd have work to do that we'd have to push into the next day, which was always a strain. But we went, no matter what—and it worked. It was a lifeline.

And the Sorrento became *our spot*. We didn't go there for every date—sometimes our dates were as simple as sitting on the front stoop of our house with a glass of wine or tea, watching the walkers and cyclists and cars pass through the neighborhood in the evening, talking about the events of the day, the things we had read or thought about, or the future. But once every couple of months, we put on our fancy clothes, went down to the Sorrento, and claimed our couch. John would bring a yellow notepad and take notes—the consummate researcher and scientist, he brought his curiosity and passion to date night as well. He'd have a list of open-ended questions to ask. Usually, we got so deep into talking about the first couple of questions that we never even made it through the list.

We all have pressures and responsibilities. We have a list of things to accomplish in a day that often is just not possible. The researchers who ran the Sloan study on working couples noted that for most people, it seemed like they had three jobs between them—the two careers, and then the incessant work of running a home and raising kids. Yes, you want to be successful at work, to show up for the people in your life, to crush your to-do list. But the bottom line is, you don't want to sacrifice your happiness in your relationship in order to do it.

That's why we are imploring people not only to keep date night on the calendar, but also to keep adventure and play alive. So many couples today have become "devitalized." And it's not just sex—it's everything. We've been drained of that energy, that life force, that electric urge to be close to one another, to be touching, to be talking, to be discovering new things about each other and, by extension, ourselves: what we want, what we dream, what we already have and appreciate. So when you want to start romance up again with a devitalized couple, it's not just opening up the bedroom. It's opening up *everything*. That's why date night isn't about where you go—or if you go anywhere at all. It's about the two of you, with no distractions.

Doing Date Night Right

Most of us hear "date," and we think *restaurant*. And yes, you can absolutely take your sweetie to a restaurant for your date! But to go on a date that matters, you do not have to get gussied up and make a reservation. In fact, we'd love it if you expanded your definition of a "date."

A date is about expanding your love maps. It's about asking open-ended questions and seeing where you end up. It's about being physically close to each other, in the same space, getting some positive touch from your partner, which is as refreshing as water is to a plant. And most importantly, dates are about *adventure*. This could be a literal adventure: going someplace new together, like sneaking into a fancy hotel. Or it might be more of a metaphorical adventure: sitting on the porch together, watching the sun set behind the trees, and seeing where the conversation takes you.

We've seen couples get incredibly inventive with dates. One couple would meet at a bar after work—but they wouldn't arrive as themselves. They would arrive in character and role-play a scenario, improvising as they sipped their happy hour cocktails. One time, he was in the KGB and she was with the CIA; they each tried to recruit the other. They did it once a month, with new characters each time. For them, it was a way to play around with identity and desire, to be imaginative and riff off each other, to find nuggets of truth in the identities they slipped on, briefly, like a coat.

Another couple who lived near an amusement park would walk there on date night, get on the Ferris wheel, and talk and laugh as the big, light-spangled wheel made its slow turn, eventually pausing them at the very top of the ride, where they could see the whole town spread out below them as they chatted about their plans for tomorrow, the weekend, or the next five years. Another, a couple who lives on Orcas Island and whose small house is often overtaken by their teenagers and their friends, would fill a backpack with candles, a bottle of wine, and cheese and apples. Then they'd walk down to the long dock that jutted out into the channel between that island and the next, spread out their picnic, and sit down there, listening to the seals clapping for fish on the water until it got too cold and the candles blew out. Even just meeting in the middle of the workday at a special park bench, eating your lunch off your knees while strangers pass by, can be a wonderful date.

Usually, our advice is to keep the date limited to just the two of you. But sometimes, it's the whole family that needs adventure. When our daughter was young, she'd get overwhelmed by her own to-do list (kids can be just like adults in this regard). One dull weekend she said to us, "I hate the weekends! All I do is homework!" So we shooed her into the car and drove down to the ferry dock in downtown Seattle, where the big green-and-white boats depart every half hour and slip across the Puget Sound to various islands and peninsulas. We didn't plan or look at the schedule. We just got in line, drove onto the next boat, and ended up wherever it took us. These impromptu adventures became a kind of tradition. Once, we arrived at a little island town full of wineries, bookshops, and galleries and wandered through the village looking at pottery and eating fudge right out of the bag. Another time, we ended up at an empty, windy beach, and we walked up and down, hunting for beach glass, laughing and yelling over the wind. It was amazing how many years we had lived in the area, just a short ferry ride away, and had never been to any of these places.

Date night does not have to be at night. It doesn't have to cost money. It doesn't have to require a babysitter. You don't even have to leave the house (although we will take you through a few important ground rules about what kinds of activities are great for date night, and which are not so great). As the pandemic stretched on, one couple, Vanessa and Carlos, took their date night to the backyard. They'd start a fire in the firepit early in the evening and let their three kids (ages two, six, and ten) roast marshmallows and eat s'mores. At bedtime, they'd stoke the fire with extra wood, put the baby to sleep, and launch the older two boys into their nighttime routine. Then they'd return to the fire outside and sit out there together—no phones, just the crackle of the wood. The kids knew that "date night" was special—that they should leave Mom and Dad alone (doing whatever it was that adults do out there by the fire with their mugs of wine, laughing about who knows what) and get themselves to bed. It never seemed to go smoothly. The boys stuck their heads out the window, whisper-screaming "Where's the toothpaste?" or "He hit me!" The baby would wake up. Sometimes it rained, but the couple would sit out there anyway, with their hoods up, laughing about it all—date night in the rain, outside under the cloudy sky, in the winter, in a pandemic.

For both, work pressures would threaten to get in the way. Vanessa was a freelance graphic artist and frequently had to push into the wee hours to meet deadlines. Carlos, a middle school math teacher, had to get up at 5:00 a.m. to grade tests before class. But at a certain point they made a pact: they wouldn't skip their once-a-week date night, no matter what.

"Yeah, I missed a couple of deadlines," says Vanessa. "It was stressful. A couple of times I got some blowback at work. But it was worth it. Something had to give. And I just decided, it wasn't going to be my marriage."

Protect It at All Costs

Many couples make a plan to start doing a regular date night, and then struggle to make it happen. When the business of life ramps up, it's the first thing on the chopping block.

Something will always try to snatch away date night: a looming work deadline, difficulty finding a babysitter, or a feeling of bone-tired exhaustion. So let us make it easy for you: *This is a requirement.* Picture us writing you a doctor's note, a prescription signed and dated, which must be urgently filled for your health. Get used to saying no to others who try to make demands on the small amount (relatively speaking!) of time you've reserved for your sweetheart.

Making a firm commitment to date night is like setting up a fortress for the two of you against the constant onslaught of the world—all the demands and deadlines and to-do tasks; the churn of chores and errands, even the deeply worthwhile pursuits that you have dedicated yourself to, whether in your career or in parenting, or both. This time is not extra. It's not a bonus or a reward. It's an investment. And the fact that it's fun does not make it frivolous. It *should* be fun. The *fun* is how date night works its magic.

A regular, nonnegotiable, come-hell-or-high-water date night is one of the interventions we recommend to couples most frequently. Why? *Because it works.* After all the data we've collected, and all the thousands of couples we've worked with one-on-one, we've seen which adjustments to the "levers" of life really make a difference—and this is one of the most powerful. If you don't have time for date night, make the time. Yes—we're suggesting that you make time. Manifest it out of thin air if you have to! Cancel something. Leave the dishes in the sink. Let the work emails wait. This is more important.

TODAY'S PRACTICE

DECLARE A DATE NIGHT— NO EXCUSES!

Today, invite your partner on a spur of the moment mini-date. A "date" doesn't have to mean a fancy dinner and a babysitter. It can happen in the backyard in the rain. It can happen on your porch.

The Ground Rules for Date Night

- No screens! No phones. No Netflix. This is real-life, human face time.

- Don't drink too much! Bonding over a glass or two of wine is just fine. But don't imbibe to the point where you're not yourself anymore.

- Make sure you're both on board with the plan! This is a joint endeavor. Everyone should be into it.

- Don't assume it's going to end in sex. Too much pressure.

- If one person needs to vent and talk about what's stressing them out, be open to that. Tonight does not have to be perfect or go in any particular way. There will be other date nights. (Like next week, since you're making this a habit, right?)

- Don't make it a social engagement. Just the two of you!

- Nervous because you haven't really talked to each other in a week, a month, a year, um . . . a decade? *Do it* anyway.

- Use some open-ended questions to get things rolling. *What's on your mind? What are you feeling happy about these days? What was your low point this week? What are you longing for right now?*

- Express interest and curiosity. *Tell me more about that. Keep going! What else happened?*

- Finally: *keep it simple.* The emphasis here is not on where you are, or how elaborate the meal. It's on conversation. Time. Touch. Intimacy. The two of you together, wherever you are.

Troubleshooting

Not sure what to do for a spontaneous, last-minute date?

Just switch up your regular routine ever so slightly for a whiff of adventure and newness. Break out a special treat you've been saving and share it. Put on some music that makes you feel close, nostalgic, festive. Especially if you're whipping up a date night at home, in your usual environment, anything that signals "*this time is different/special*" will help put up a protective bubble around the intimate space of date night.

Julie says: "My parents used to have a date where they'd turn off all the lights, light candles, and sit on the living room floor and eat at the coffee table—just for something different and romantic."

And if you feel like it, dress up! Even if you're not leaving the house. Put on your nice clothes and get out the fancy glasses. Why not? It brings a special-occasion air to even the most mundane of weeknights.

RENEWING YOUR PRESCRIPTION

TY AND OLLIE HAVE BEEN TOGETHER FOR TWO YEARS. TY IS FROM CAL-
ifornia, and Ollie's from Nigeria, though he grew up in London,
where he and Ty now live together in a small flat. Both men are
in their early twenties. In the grand scheme of things, their relationship is brand-new. But they've already figured out some
of the secrets of success that we see in the "masters" of love.

When these two lovebirds were less than one year into their
relationship, one of the most influential events of our lifetimes
began to unfold: the COVID-19 pandemic. Suddenly, they were
no longer going out on dates, meeting up with friends, traveling,
exploring the city. They were in their small apartment together,
24/7, learning to do their jobs remotely, learning to be in a full-
time, full-on, all-day/all-night relationship.

Ty says one of the first things that popped up was their different conflict styles. Ty's natural tendency was to avoid or shy
away from direct confrontation; Ollie's was to talk it out immediately.

"We'd have some moment of friction over who knows what—you know there are plenty of those!" Ty says. "My natural tendency was to be like, 'Oh, I'll just bottle that up and hold a grudge. But Ollie would just chase me down and talk it out with me. Whatever it was we'd been fighting about would just be . . . neutralized. Like it didn't have any power over us anymore. I'd never had that kind of pattern in a relationship before. It feels really good."

They have figured out other stuff, too. How to give each other space. How to do their own thing without pressure from the other partner to do exactly what he's doing (critical, in a pandemic lockdown!). How to find time to set aside work and social media and other demands and connect with *just each other*. Their jobs don't line up wonderfully for this: Ty's job is on California time; Ollie's, on London time. Ollie starts early; Ty, in the afternoon. Ty often has to work through dinner, or he says, "I sit there eating with my phone open, tapping out email replies." So how do they spend *quality* time together?

"We stay up really late," Ty says. "We make our own schedule. We're night owls. We're up, chatting and playing video games and talking about the future, when most people are asleep."

In the middle of a busy day, if they feel like they need a moment of micro-connection to realign, one will ask the other for a long hug or a "thirty-second lie-down"—so, between Zoom calls, they'll lie down and spoon for less than a minute. It's like supercharging a battery.

The biggest challenge for Ty and Ollie—who are at the begin-

ning of what they hope will be a long journey together—is figuring out how to have space for their needs, desires, and dreams
while also navigating expectations, worries about independence,
and more.

"I'd be sitting at my desk writing, having a fantasy about moving to Barcelona, renting a sunny apartment, walking the cob-
blestone streets, meeting people, and just being a young guy
alone in a city," Ty says.

In his past relationships, his partners didn't have great responses to this kind of thing. Ty was loath to bring it up at the
risk of a big fight, bad feelings, insecurity, and jealousy.

"I had some not nice relationships," Ty says. "But with Ollie,
I just brought it up. I didn't want to have all this lurking stuff
we weren't talking about. So I said, 'If I wanted to go to Barcelona without you for a month, would you be OK with that?' and
he basically said, 'Of course, if that's what you need.'"

They had a big talk. Ty, reflecting on himself, says he thinks
all the time about the different lives he could lead—all the possible paths sprouting off from one another, like a tree with infinite splitting branches. He loves Ollie and their life together.
But he also longs to be able to explore on his own—to be an au-
tonomous person in the world.

"There's always going to be a part of me that craves that—the
individualized experience," he says. "But Ollie has made space
for it. I can have these whims. I can feel like I have space to
move. I can explore these possibilities without him feeling hurt.
We can be individuals. Because we can talk about this stuff

openly, I realized that being in a relationship doesn't have to hold me back from doing what I want to do. I can do it while having a home base."

As we were writing this book, Ty and Ollie were looking forward to quarantine restrictions being lifted. Soon they'd be able to travel again. They were making plans to visit Ty's family in California. But for the moment, they were going strong. They celebrated their two-year anniversary in pandemic lockdown. They couldn't do the kind of anniversary date they normally would do, like go to Gordon Ramsay's restaurant and drink fancy cocktails at a crowded bar. They had to make some anniversary magic at home. While Ty was making dinner, he heard all kinds of rummaging around in the living room. "Don't come out here yet!" Ollie shouted.

The big reveal: Ollie had built . . . a fort. He'd pushed the couches together, stacked up the cushions, draped the whole soft castle in pretty blankets. In the middle, he'd created a whole picnic setup, complete with a bottle of wine and nice glasses.

It was a fun and fresh anniversary, despite the pandemic. But these two say that the main thing that keeps them great friends and lovers, even through one of the most turbulent and unpredictable times any of us has ever been through, is that they appreciate each other, all day long.

"All day long, we constantly say at every opportunity we have, 'Thank you, I appreciate you, you're wonderful to me,'" Ty says. "We say thank you for everything, big or little. For listening to an emotional venting. For making a cup of coffee when he makes himself one. For everything. And we mean it, and feel it, every time."

Matt and Adrienne live halfway across the globe from Ty and Ollie and have been married for forty-four years—since long before those two were born. They have two children and three grandchildren. And yet, Adrienne says now that she never intended to marry or have kids. If you were to go back in time and tell her that she and Matt would still be married more than four decades later, she would have found it hard to believe.

"It was the seventies," Adrienne says, when they met and fell in love. "Nobody was getting married! It wasn't cool. Plus, I watched my mother stay home and raise five kids. None of the women in my mother's generation had careers. When I left home to go to college, I didn't know what I wanted to do, but I knew two things for sure: I was never getting married. And I was never having kids."

She met Matt in 1974 while working at the student newspaper in college. He was the photo editor, and she worked in the composing room, laying out the copy. He would come in, gaze at her, ask for a date—she always said no. Then she bumped into him at a Halloween party, where he showed up dressed as a mad scientist, with wild hair and a mischievous grin, and she had a change of heart. Standing above him on the house stairs as he chatted with other costumed partygoers drinking keg beer out of SOLO cups, she kicked off one of her shoes, reached her foot down, and ran her toes through his hair.

"It was," she says, "quite a moment!"

Two years later, he asked her to marry him. She said no. No one she knew was getting married. It didn't seem like marriage was really in a woman's best interest. But he kept asking. And finally, wanting to make him happy, she agreed.

"I thought, 'Well, why not—I can always get a divorce!'"

They got married at city hall at nine o'clock in the morning, with their parents for witnesses. He wore a navy cardigan. She wore a blouse and skirt. No wedding rings.

The years that followed were full of ups and downs. Adrienne was a graphic artist, but gave it up when her children came along. It was too hard, she found, to both parent an infant and work—especially with Matt's long hours commuting into the city, a four-hour train ride round trip. It was a sacrifice. They moved, several times, for his jobs. She felt like she was giving up too much, but mostly didn't talk about it.

"The years when the kids were young were the hardest," Adrienne says. "He worked long hours and had an exhausting commute. We lived far from our families and I never got a break from childcare. And I'd fallen into this traditional arrangement that I'd always said I never wanted. I realize now that I never talked to him back then about how little support I was getting from him. I didn't tell him what I needed from him. I just stewed silently for years."

For his part, Matt was having his own struggles trying to establish himself in a cutthroat corporate workplace. He says now, "I just put my head down and charged. I did focus on my career. The responsibility of providing for a family kept me awake at night. But I didn't share my challenges at the time, either."

Since then, Matt has changed careers to one he finds more fulfilling in the public service realm. No longer consumed by raising children, Adrienne has more freedom to pursue her own career, launching a freelance business and returning to the graphic design she was doing pre-motherhood. They both say their relationship is better than ever, and now a source of refuge and support. But that didn't happen overnight.

It came gradually, from small course corrections, like letting little stuff go. Talking about needs and issues as they came up, instead of stewing on them. And they started prioritizing time together, to just go out and have fun. They go on adventures almost every weekend: a hike in the woods, a drive to an outdoor sculpture park, a picnic in the snow. They head off on bike rides on a rail trail to a bookstore that Adrienne loves, then stop at Matt's favorite vintage diner for lunch on the way back. Every year on their anniversary, they do the same thing: they take a bottle of champagne into the woods, find a place with a lovely view to sit, and share a toast. Even in the rain.

Both describe the arc of their relationship as two sets of train tracks—running together, closely in tandem; other times split apart and parallel; then intersecting again. There were times they wondered if they would make it. There was no big revelation that kept them together. There was just the daily work of deciding, moment to moment, that their marriage was worth it, and that they chose it, again and again. Being able to communicate more openly with each other has been huge. They have, at long last, shared their earlier struggles with each other. Each has a far more accurate picture of those harder years, and what it was like for the other person; they see how they shut each other out, and how that made things even tougher. Adrienne says she doesn't hold back on sharing her feelings anymore—they are both more vocal about what they're going through, thinking, and feeling, which nips resentments and misunderstandings in the bud.

"They said it would never last," she says. "No, really— everybody said it right to our faces: *It will never last*. Well, guess what, it did."

What have they learned in forty-four years of marriage?

"That you always have to be remeeting each other," Adrienne says. "You're not the same person at sixty that you were at twenty. It's not possible. So you have to notice when you've lost track of each other—it happens. I don't know that you can be together for a lifetime and not experience that. The question is, do you make the effort to get to know each other again? Are you curious? Can you stay friends? That's what romance is, really. It's friendship."

You've Come a Long Way This Week!

Over the past week, as you worked through this book, you introduced seven new relationship-building habits into each day. You practiced the key habits of the true masters of love:

- You set aside time to check in with each other, asking "What do you need from me today?" *Keep going*: make sure your schedule moving forward continues to involve healthy routines of connection.

- You asked each other big, open-ended questions, questions that hopefully took you into new territory, where you learned something you didn't already know about your partner. *Keep going:* remember that we're not only creating love maps but also *updating* them. When it comes to your partner, their inner landscape will always be changing. And that's what makes it so exciting to know someone intimately for a long time.

- You noticed what your partner was doing right and said thank you for something routine. *Keep going:* Expressing appreciation is not a one-time job you can check off and be done with. Expressing gratitude and receiving appreciation is an emotional lift that can buoy you both, every day.

- You gave your partner a heartfelt compliment. *Keep going:* Admiration is something you actively do. Everybody has flaws, and we all get frustrated with one another. But you can choose to balance that out and to keep a sturdy foundation of mutual respect and admiration under your feet by remembering to focus on what's wonderful, unique, and irreplaceable about this person you are lucky enough to share a life with.

- You practiced telling your partner what you need—*before* an unexpressed need or desire becomes a source of resentment. *Keep going:* stay ten steps ahead of resentment by expressing your needs, wants, and hopes when you feel them.

- You made it a point to sneak in more sweet intimate moments of physical touch. *Keep going:* Physical touch and closeness are great for your health, your connection, and your sex life.

Hold hands. Kiss for no reason. Move in for a hug. Your future self, who will probably have better blood pressure and a stronger relationship, will thank you!

- And finally, you declared a spontaneous date. *Keep going*: don't stop dating each other—ever! And while spontaneous dates like the one you had this week are great, the best dating advice we can give you is to plan ahead, set a time every week for date night, line up whatever support you need (such as a babysitter), and be militant about protecting it. We are so passionate about couples having date night regularly and right that we wrote a whole book about it called *Eight Dates: Essential Conversations for a Lifetime of Love*. If you enjoyed this week of practices and want to take the next step, we recommend this one next!

Here's our hope for you, after this week: That you felt a little closer to your partner after including these practices in your day. That you two laughed together at some point. That you felt that warm glow of connection, the *cha-ching!* of coins dropping into the emotional bank account. Maybe you even had a conversation or conflict this week where you were able to draw on that "money in the bank," and it went a little smoother than usual.

We talked earlier about the Four Horsemen—criticism, contempt, defensiveness, and stonewalling—those destructive forces that can come galloping into a relationship when we forget how important these small things are, when they get brushed aside in favor of life's business and pressures, when they cease to be *habits*. Your mission now is to make these practices as routine as brushing your teeth—to solidify them as habits that are a natural part of the rhythm of your day. When you do this, you're putting a suit of armor on your relationship that the Four Horsemen cannot breach. You're making your relationship bulletproof.

By making and maintaining these small changes, you and your partner can entirely change your trajectory. Picture it like this:

Those lines start out far apart. And their angle changes by only a fraction of a degree as you move from left to right. But inevitably, they come together! John calls this "convergent accelerating trajectories." Translation: greater change over time through "small things often."

So, to solidify your convergent accelerating trajectories, we'd like to ask you to do two things as you move forward from this week:

1. Write down your observations.

We know, from testing out these interventions on real couples in the lab and in the wild, that these habits truly work to strengthen relationships. But each couple is different. As you tried out these new techniques this week, you may have noticed that some hit home right away. Others you may need to keep trying, and give them a little time to work their magic. One way you can help that process along is by paying attention to the impact these new little habits have on you and your relationship, and by writing it down to track it.

At the end of this book, we've provided space for a short and sweet daily journal. Moving forward from today, we'd love for you to begin keeping some notes, at the end of each day, on how you feel you've been changing—both you individually (your lens on the world, how you see and experience your day) and the two of you as a couple. Every night, spare a few minutes to flip to the back of this book (or use a separate notebook or journal if you prefer) and jot down a few notes about the small changes you've been making and how they feel.

It takes only a minute or two, but the data you gather can be invaluable. Maybe some of these practices didn't do anything revolutionary for you on the single day you tried it. But when you incorporate it into your routine regularly, you'll see the difference. Keeping some notes on your experience will let you see which practices have a big impact over time—you won't be able to miss it.

2. Have a mini "State of the Union" meeting.

Once a week for the next month, have a short meeting, just the two of you, on the weekend (or whatever time off you share). We call this meeting the "State of the Union" because your job is to talk only about what's gone *right* in your relationship. What felt good this week, between the two of you? Just share that with each other. And think of three specific things you appreciated about your partner this week, and tell them. For example: *I really appreciate how you cleaned the kitchen the other night when I was so tired, without me even asking—it made me feel so taken care of.*

There are plenty of opportunities every day to notice what's not right, undone, imperfect. Your job at your weekly State of the Union is to recap all your successes, your highs, your ups. You give yourself a weekly dose of positivity and mutual appreciation—a love high five.

An additional resource we'd love to point you toward is our free app, Gottman Card Decks, which is full of additional questions and prompts that will help you continue to work on all of the practices we've covered this week. We built the app based on the actual card decks we use with couples during our "Art and Science of Love" weekend workshops, but we wanted them to be available to anyone. The app has a variety of decks of questions for you to choose from, including Date Questions, Open-Ended Questions, Expressing Needs, and more. If you want a free, no-strings-attached, easy way to spark conversation and build love maps, this is a great tool to have—literally!—in your back pocket.

We want to leave you with this final thought: *Love is worth it.* It's worth taking the time, even on the busiest, most chaotic of days, to turn toward your partner instead of barreling on with your to-do list. To sit down together in the middle of all the chaos and talk. To miss a deadline in order to go on a date. *It's worth it.*

Good relationships strengthen everything. They boost your mood. They give you a solid bedrock from which to tackle your day, your goals, your dreams. They bring down the amount of stress hormones in your body. They even strengthen your immune system. They counteract all those things that can shorten our lives or make them less vibrant: loneliness, depression, disease. There are all these hidden benefits to a positive relationship that we often don't think about, or even really know about. But the science is clear: good relationships lengthen your life and make it even more worth living.

So yes, our days are busy. It never feels like there's enough time for everything. But love is the important thing—the thing that makes everything else more possible. And as we hope you've seen this week, you don't need swaths of extra time to invest in your relationship. You just need a little bit of time, every day. A small investment that multiplies over time: compound interest.

Remember that Nina Simone line: "I want a little sugar in my bowl"? We like to think about it this way: The relationship is a cup of tea you can flavor however you choose. And you can choose to put a little sugar into that cup, instead of salt. When you're wounded, or raw, or tired, salt hurts. It's grating, it stings. Sugar makes you feel better. It washes away that sting and bitterness. That's all you're really doing, when you add these small things into your day: putting a little sugar into your relationship, to make it sweeter and sweeter.

THE SMALL
THINGS JOURNAL

Moving forward from this week, we'd love for you to begin keeping some notes, at the end of each day, on how you feel you've been changing—both you individually and the two of you as a couple. Every night, spare a few minutes to jot down some notes about the small positive changes you've been making, the small positive changes your partner has been making, how these changes make you feel, and if you noticed any impact on your relationship from these changes. It takes only a minute or two, but the data you gather can be invaluable. Maybe some of these practices didn't do anything revolutionary for you on the single day you tried it. But when you incorporate it into your routine regularly, you'll see the difference. When you run out of room here, continue the practice in a separate notebook or journal. Keeping some notes on your experience will let you see which practices have a big impact over time—you won't be able to miss it.

THE SMALL THINGS JOURNAL

ACKNOWLEDGMENTS

We want to thank Doug Abrams, visionary founder of Idea Architects, and his brilliant wife, Dr. Rachel Carlton Abrams, who have honored us with their friendship and devotion to doing good in the world. You both are life-changers for millions, and for us. This book could not have been written without the eloquent wordsmithing of Alyssa Knickerbocker, the editing and leadership of Rachel Neumann, Lara Love, and the terrific work of the entire IA team.

We are also eternally grateful to Edward Sargent, who has taken over the helm of the Gottman Institute with incisive clear-eyed leadership and skill. Thank you, Captain P., our trusted dear friend. In addition, thanks go to our Institute's research director, Carrie Cole, and our clinical director, Donald Cole, who are not only brilliant psychologists but also our cherished Seattle housemates and friends. Thank you for supporting us throughout the writing of this book. Profound thanks also go to the entire Institute team, without whom we'd still be cave dwelling in our offices.

We want to give kudos and our deep appreciation to Rafael Lisitsa, our dear friend, cofounder, and treasured leader of Affective Software, Inc. (ASI), a sister company of the Gottman Institute that has created a web-based platform and new home for all our relationship work. Profound gratitude also goes to Vladimir Brayman, chief technology officer of ASI, whose energy, dedication, and wondrous brain power are beyond measure. Thanks also to the entire ASI team, especially Inna Brayman, Connor Eaton, and Steven Fan, who have helped us to create and clarify the tools found here.

We also acknowledge our closest friends who have supported us throughout our writing of this book: Alison Shaw and Dick Jager, Phil and Cara Cohn, Mavis Tsai, and Lana Lisitsa. This book's content would have been impossible to create without John's five decades of friendship and close collaboration with Robert Levenson. Thank you, all.

Finally, we extend our deepest love and gratitude to Moriah, Steven, and Ezra Fan-Gottman, who show us daily how beautiful love and family can be.

NOTES

INTRODUCTION: SMALL THINGS OFTEN

1. Kim T. Buehlman, John M. Gottman, Lynn F. Katz, "How a Couple Views Their Past Predicts Their Future: Predicting Divorce from an Oral History Interview," *Journal of Family Psychology* 5, nos. 3–4 (1992): 295–318.

HOW TO USE THIS BOOK

1. John Gottman, *What Predicts Divorce? The Relationship Between Marital Processes and Marital Outcomes* (Hillsdale, NJ: Lawrence Erlbaum Associates, 1994).
2. John Gottman, *The Relationship Cure* (New York: Three Rivers Press, 2001).
3. Belinda Campos et al., "Positive and Negative Emotion in the Daily Life of Dual-Earner Couples with Children," *Journal of Family Psychology* 27, no. 1 (2013): 76–85, accessed November 29, 2021, https://doi.org/10.1037/a0031413.

DAY 1: MAKE CONTACT

1. John Gottman, *What Predicts Divorce? The Relationship Between Marital Processes and Marital Outcomes* (Hillsdale, NJ: Lawrence Erlbaum Associates, 1994).

2. Julia C. Babcock et al., "A Component Analysis of a Brief Psycho-educational Couples' Workshop: One-Year Follow-up Results," *Journal of Family Therapy* 35, no. 3 (2013): 252–80, accessed November 29, 2021, https://doi.org/10.1111/1467-6427.12017.

DAY 2: ASK A BIG QUESTION

1. Unpublished finding from a survey of a workshop done with more than five hundred couples through the Gottman Institute.

DAY 3: SAY THANK YOU

1. Elizabeth A. Robinson and Gail M. Price, "Pleasurable Behavior in Marital Interaction: An Observational Study," *Journal of Consulting and Clinical Psychology* 48, no. 1 (1980): 117–18, accessed December 2, 2021, https://doi.org/10.1037/0022-006X.48.1.117.

2. Robert Weiss, "Strategic Behavioral Relationship Therapy: A Model for Assessment and Intervention," in *Advances in Family Intervention, Assessment, and Theory*, vol. 1, ed. J. P. Vincent (Greenwich, CT: JAI Process, 1980): 229–71.

3. Richard Davidson and Sharon Begley, *The Emotional Life of Your Brain* (New York: Hudson Street Press, 2012).

4. Richard J. Davidson and Antoine Lutz, "Buddha's Brain: Neuroplasticity and Meditation," *IEEE Signal Process Mag* 25, no. 1 (2008): 174–76, accessed December 2, 2021, doi:10.1109/msp.2008.4431873.

5. Renay P. Cleary Bradley, Daniel J. Friend, and John M. Gottman, "Supporting Healthy Relationships in Low-Income, Violent Couples: Reducing Conflict and Strengthening Relationship Skills and Satisfaction," *Journal of Couple & Relationship Therapy* 10, no. 2 (2011): 97–116, accessed December 2, 2021, http://dx.doi.org/10.1080/15332691.2011.562808.

6. "Mental Health Disorder Statistics," Johns Hopkins Medicine, accessed February 4, 2022, www.hopkinsmedicine.org/health/wellness-and-prevention/mental-health-disorder-statistics.

7. Jillian McKoy, "Depression Rates in US Tripled When the Pandemic First Hit—Now, They're Even Worse," *The Brink*, Boston University,

October 7, 2021, https://www.bu.edu/articles/2021/depression-rates -tripled-when-pandemic-first-hit.

DAY 4: GIVE A REAL COMPLIMENT

1. John Gottman, *What Predicts Divorce? The Relationship Between Marital Processes and Marital Outcomes* (Hillsdale, NJ: Lawrence Erlbaum Associates, 1994).
2. John M. Gottman and Julie Schwartz Gottman, *The Science of Couples and Family Therapy: Behind the Scenes at the Love Lab* (New York: W. W. Norton, 2018).
3. Gottman and Gottman, *The Science of Couples*.
4. John M. Gottman and Clifford I. Notarius, "Marital Research in the 20th Century and a Research Agenda for the 21st Century," *Family Process* 41, no. 2 (2002): 159–97, accessed December 2, 2021, https://doi .org/10.1111/j.1545-5300.2002.41203.x.
5. John M. Gottman et al., "Predicting Marital Happiness and Stability from Newlywed Interactions," *Journal of Marriage and Family* 60, no. 1 (1998): 5–22, accessed December 2, 2021, https://www.jstor.org /stable/353438.
6. Gottman et al., "Predicting Marital Happiness."
7. John M. Gottman and Robert W. Levenson, "Marital Interaction: Physiological Linkage and Affective Exchange," *Journal of Personality and Social Psychology* 45, no. 3 (1983): 587–97.
8. John M. Gottman and Robert W. Levenson, "Physiological and Affective Predictors of Change in Relationship Satisfaction," *Journal of Personality and Social Psychology* 49, no. 1 (1985): 85–94.

DAY 5: ASK FOR WHAT YOU NEED

1. Sybil Carrère and John M. Gottman, "Predicting Divorce among Newlyweds from the First Three Minutes of a Marital Conflict Discussion," *Family Process* 38, no. 3 (1999): 293–301, accessed December 2, 2021, https://doi.org/10.1111/j.1545-5300.1999.00293.x.
2. John M. Gottman, *What Predicts Divorce? The Relationship Between*

Marital Processes and Marital Outcomes (Hillsdale, NJ: Lawrence Erlbaum Associates, 1994).

DAY 6: REACH OUT AND TOUCH

1. Chrisanna Northrup, Pepper Schwartz, and James Witte, *The Normal Bar: The Surprising Secrets of Happy Couples and What They Reveal About Creating a New Normal in Your Relationship* (New York: Harmony Books, 2013).

2. Paul Zak, *The Moral Molecule: The Source of Love and Prosperity* (New York: Dutton, 2021).

3. Ashley Montagu, *Touching: The Human Significance of Skin* (New York: Harper & Row, 1986), 87.

4. Maham Hasan, "What All That Touch Deprivation Is Doing to Us," *New York Times*, October 6, 2020, https://www.nytimes.com/2020/10/06/style/touch-deprivation-coronavirus.html.

5. Tiffany Field, *Touch* (Cambridge, MA: MIT Press, 2001).

6. Sheldon Cohen et al., "Does Hugging Provide Stress-Buffering Social Support? A Study of Susceptibility to Upper Respiratory Infection and Illness," *Psychological Science* 26, no. 2 (2015): 135–47, accessed December 2, 2021, https://doi.org/10.1177/0956797614559284.

7. Tiffany Field, "Touch Therapy Effects on Development," *International Journal of Behavioral Development* 22, no. 4 (1998): 779–97; Tiffany Field, Miguel Diego, and Mari Hernandez-Reif, "Preterm Infant Massage Therapy Research: A Review," *Infant Behavior and Development* 33, no. 2 (2011): 115–24, accessed December 2, 2021, https://doi.org/10.1016/j.infbeh.2009.12.004.

8. Alyson F. Shapiro et al., "Bringing Baby Home Together: Examining the Impact of a Couple-Focused Intervention on the Dynamics within Family Play," *American Journal of Orthopsychiatry* 8, no. 3 (2011): 337–50.

9. Sidney M. Jourard, "An Exploratory Study of Body-Accessibility," *British Journal of Social and Clinical Psychology* 5, no. 3 (1966): 221–31, accessed December 2, 2021, https://doi.org/10.1111/j.2044-8260.1966.tb00978.x.

10. Terri D. Fisher, Zachary T. Moore, and Mary-Jo Pittenger, "Sex on the Brain?: An Examination of Frequency of Sexual Cognitions as a Func-

tion of Gender, Erotophilia, and Social Desirability," *Journal of Sex Research* 49, no. 1 (2012): 69–77, accessed February 7, 2022, doi:10.1080/00224499.2011.565429.

11. Caleb E. Finch, "Evolution of the Human Lifespan and Diseases of Aging: Roles of Infection, Inflammation, and Nutrition," *PNAS* 107, no. 1 (2010): 1718–24, accessed December 2, 2021, https://doi.org/10.1073/pnas.0909606106.

12. James A. Coan, Hillary S. Schaefer, and Richard J. Davison, "Lending a Hand: Social Regulation of the Neural Response to Threat," *Psychological Science* 17, no. 12 (2006): 1032–39, accessed December 2, 2021, https://doi.org/10.1111/j.1467-9280.2006.01832.x.

13. James A. Coan et al., "Relationship Status and Perceived Support in the Social Regulation of Neural Responses to Threat," *Social Cognitive and Affective Neuroscience* 12, no. 10 (2017): 1574–83, accessed December 2, 2021, https://doi.org/10.1093/scan/nsx091.

14. Paul J. Zak, Angela A. Stanton, and Sheila Ahmadi, "Oxytocin Increases Generosity in Humans," *PLoS ONE* 2, no. 11 (2007): e1128, https://doi.org/10.1371/journal.pone.0001128.

15. Paul J. Zak, "The Neurobiology of Trust," *Scientific American* 298, no. 6 (2008): 88–95, accessed December 2, 2021, http://www.jstor.org/stable/26000645.

16. Zak, *The Moral Molecule*.

17. Sheril Kirshenbaum, *The Science of Kissing: What Our Lips Are Telling Us* (New York: Grand Central Publishing, 2011).

18. Samantha A. Wagner et al., "Touch Me Just Enough: The Intersection of Adult Attachment, Intimate Touch, and Marital Satisfaction," *Journal of Social and Personal Relationships* 37, no. 6 (2020): 1945–67, accessed December 2, 2021, https://doi.org/10.1177/0265407520910791.

19. John M. Gottman, *What Predicts Divorce? The Relationship Between Marital Processes and Marital Outcomes* (Hillsdale, NJ: Lawrence Erlbaum Associates, 1994).

DAY 7: DECLARE A DATE NIGHT

1. The Sloan study was the first of its kind. Belinda Campos et al., "Positive and Negative Emotion in the Daily Life of Dual-Earner Couples with

Children," *Journal of Family Psychology* 27, no. 1 (2013): 76–85, accessed November 29, 2021, https://doi.org/10.1037/a0031413; Lynn Smith, "Two Incomes, with Kids and a Scientist's Camera," *CELF in the News*, UCLA Center on Everyday Lives of Families, July 29, 2001, http://www.celf.ucla.edu/pages/news1.html; Benedict Cary, "Families' Every Fuss, Archived and Analyzed," *New York Times,* May 22, 2010, https://www.nytimes.com/2010/05/23/science/23family.html.

2. John M. Gottman et al., "Gay, Lesbian, and Heterosexual Couples About to Begin Couples Therapy: An Online Relationship Assessment of 40,681 Couples," *Journal of Marital and Family Therapy* 46, no. 2 (2020): 218–39, https://doi.org/10.1111/jmft.12395.

3. Michele Weiner-Davis, *The Sex-Starved Marriage* (New York: Simon & Schuster, 2003).

THE LOVE PRESCRIPTION

Seven Days to More Intimacy, Connection, and Joy

For the past forty years, Drs. John Gottman and Julie Schwartz Gottman have been studying love. They've gathered data on over three thousand couples, looking at everything from their body language to the way they converse to their stress hormone levels. Their goal: identify the building blocks of love.

THE SLEEP PRESCRIPTION

Seven Days to Unlocking Your Best Rest

Sleep is as essential as food, water, and oxygen. So how can something that should be so instinctual and automatic be so hard? Dr. Aric Prather runs one of the world's most successful sleep clinics and has cracked the code to help even the most restless of sleepers get a good night's rest.

THE STRESS PRESCRIPTION

Seven Days to More Joy and Ease

While we can't eliminate stress altogether, what we *can* change is our response to it. Dr. Elissa Epel has dedicated her career to studying stress. And what she's learned over years of research is that the secret to tackling stress is not simply to avoid it—it's to experience stress *differently*.

PENGUIN BOOKS

Ready to find your next great read? Let us help. Visit prh.com/nextread